Above the
TURBULENCE

Above the
TURBULENCE

Your Ticket Out of Pain To Purpose

CAROLYN DECK

ISBN: 979-8-88759-703-4 - paperback
ISBN: 979-8-88759-704-1 - ebook

Independently published by Carolyn Deck

For more information, signed copies, and bulk orders, email c.deck4405@gmail.com.

Cover designer: Jeanly Zamora
Editor: Margaret A. Harrell, https://margaretharrell.com

This book is dedicated to the one, the one child from shattered beginnings. Now grown…still in the debris? Take hope. To those, Faces with Names, may you thrive and fulfill your God-given purpose. For this is a message of the Father's heart to you. Out of the darkness into the light, to grow newness of self and life, living a hope-filled future until you reach your final destination.

CONTENTS

INTRODUCTION

Our Choices Change Everything. Life is just fine one day then out of nowhere, we're caught completely off guard—a windy road with its blind corners and potholes appears, taking us off course. Difficulties and trials are our unwanted travel mates. Some, we never invited and certainly never saw coming, while others if we are honest, we brought along ourselves through poor choices.

How we respond defines us and ultimately brings us to our destiny.

This book is a practical, no-holds-barred guide to what's worked for me, resulting in a transformed life; a healthier, authentic me; loving, honest relationships, with a hope-filled, *fearless* future. You can have this, too. It is as simple as saying yes and taking the next step.

Knowing our roots, how our past shaped us, and why we behave as we do moves us ahead on the path of understanding. We then face more questions: *Is this the road I want to travel? Can I change my mind, how I think, what I believe? Can I really learn to behave differently and revise my destiny?* The answer is yes.

I was that kid, growing up in a broken home. Oh, the pain of watching my parents fight, hearing them shout. Each incident tore at my young heart—the angry, malicious words tossed around like a lost boat at sea. Scared, afraid, insecure, lonely, I was stuck living in the only home I knew. Then, with no warning, at a family meeting I heard the decision loud and clear: "We'll take her." I was to leave. (I go further into this tale of my abrupt uprooting in Chapter 1.)

Moving into a new home was life changing. It made me realize the universal truth that nothing is static; we have choices. It was all-important, how I responded, knowing I alone was responsible.

Stop for a moment and ask yourself this: *What is the truth about my life and the decisions I've made?* Have you ever struggled to accept the consequences, even to admit them? If you're anything like me, some were hard to handle. What was your reaction? Shock, guilt, remorse, resentment, anger, bitterness? Can you learn from these insights, understanding how to use even those broken, fragmented pieces of your past constructively?

The ongoing pain of brokenness is costly. Mired in my mind, my focus clouded, the lies I'd told myself—heard them in my mind as a child: "I'm hopeless. My future looks bleak. I have no way out"—rang like truths to me.

Entangled in the stress and turmoil, I experienced firsthand the splintered relationship of my parents. Carrying around their emotional baggage as excess luggage weighed them down. As with the pebble dropped in a pond, the ripple effect was far reaching into surrounding lives. Into my life.

> *My past gave me the lens to examine why I'd made the choices I did; I saw how experiences shaped me and that **how I responded was the key to where I ended up***

Years later, I realized, though, that my past gave me the lens to examine why I'd made the choices I did; I saw how experiences shaped me and that *how I responded was the key to where I ended up*—pivotal to the outcome. Like an air-traffic controller, I started directing the lies to leave. Slowly but surely, I ditched my excess luggage. I felt victorious as I surrendered my thoughts, shifting how I saw myself, my family, my life, and God.

G.O.D. (Getting Out of the Disaster) set me free. A new journey began. What was true was what I embraced from then on; the rest, I had no use for. I focused on what I could control—my thoughts—resulting in better choices. No longer dwelling in the past, I gained the strength and courage to face each new challenge—with extraordinary results, well beyond what I ever thought possible.

My trials are my testimony to you: How to travel above the turbulence *is* achievable.

I will show you how, but first, I have some more questions for you:

1: Can you be honest with yourself?
2: Are you willing to change, or do you want "safe and same"?
3: Do you want a better way for your life, spilling over into better health, relationships, and happiness?

If you have answered *yes* to these questions, *great*. I'm excited for you. I have the answers. So, ready to travel?

The above intro covers the focus of Part One. But then there is a surprise. The unique thing about this book is that not only does it show you how to navigate life's turbulence, but also it is a travel book. As a former travel agent, I have loads of travel tips for you along with travel stories that illustrate the message above.

Part One

Oh yes, You shaped me first inside, then out;
you formed me in my mother's womb.
You know me inside and out. You know every bone in
my body. You know exactly how I was made, bit by bit,
how I was sculpted from nothing into something.
Psalm 139:13,15 (MSG)

This verse is the substance of life by which I live and breathe. It is my comfort and strength knowing my Heavenly Father made me and He cares about me and for me.

My beginning started with love; then something changed.

1

Messy Turbulent Start— No Love Boat Cruise

My journey, as do most journeys, started at home. I had a big sister, a mum, and a dad. My mum worked part-time as a nurse, and Dad was *always* busy with work, church, or the Boys' Brigade—a Christian-based Boy Scouts. He wasn't around much. I'd walk to school with my sister, occasionally play at a friend's house after school, do homework, have dinner, and go to bed. Repeat. My simple, normal life. Dad disapproved of television; he was very against having that box, with its black-and-white images, in our living room, talking rubbish and wasting our time. I can't honestly remember how I spent my time at home. Sadly, what springs to my mind is the turbulence. The cracks formed, then opened to giant chasms; it had once been a warm home (singing around the piano, Dad playing guitar, card games, fun, and laughter).

Then my shalom got invaded. Icy voids of heartache emerged, as more frequently, Mum and Dad's discussions escalated into full-scale arguments. Like a fire hydrant, the full force of angry words would scream out into what had been a peaceful home. Then the physical push and shove started. I could hear the thud as my parents fought over the phone hanging on the wall. Mum would reach for the receiver to dial 111 (the police), and Dad, in his strength, would throw her off balance. Petrified, I'd go into hiding. Occasionally, Mum made the call, and the boys in blue appeared. Tall men in police uniforms would run down our steps from the road to our front door. The police were always calm, talking gently, de-escalating the situation. That was all it took. Words used for good.

> *calm, talking gently, de-escalating the situation. That was all it took. Words used for good.*

The pain of two broken people was clear for my young eyes to witness. Mum started drinking more, forgetting where she last hid her half-empty bottle. I'd find it behind the curtain. The glass stains lingering on the end of the piano bore witness to her pain.

Dad seemed incapable of talking through conflicts with Mum.

Choosing to escape the scene and avoid the issues, he'd spend most nights back at the office. If it wasn't work that required his time, it was his Boys' Brigade. After work, he'd give a group of struggling kids his tips and tricks on how to study and sit for exams.

That always puzzled me, given I was so lousy at both. Perhaps I should have invited myself to those sessions. Being a tomboy, I'd have fitted in.

What a turbulent mess. Yep, it sucked. My younger days as a child were tough, even unfair. My parents had no fairy tale love story. Hurting people resulted in hurt people. Me. Their choices and responses affected my life. My shalom was no more. So many questions. Why could Dad not be the head of the house? Why did he go out each night? Why did Mum choose to drink so much? Why couldn't my parents just work it out? Why would two grown people behave this way?

Reflection:

How have you dealt with the crap choices of others invading your life?

How have your responses affected you?

How long are you prepared to keep walking the same path?

Keep reading. There are good choices to be made.

2

What to Know Is the Fuel to Go

"We'll have her."

Wait. What?

That was all I remember hearing. It was the beginning of the end. The end of my family as I'd known it. My future, out of *my* control—it was about to change.

As I peered around the kitchen door, keeping out of sight, there sat my family: my older sister, the one who'd always looked out for me as all good big sisters do, and my two parents. Mum's head hung low, while Dad's emotionless face stared across the table. Our little dining room, with barely space for a wooden table and four chairs, still smelt of eggs and toast: our standard breakfast menu. Thanks, Dad. He was always about starting our day well.

"Carolyn can't stay on living here. Your mother isn't up to it."

Judging words or realistic? Both, actually. As the discussions continued, my name came up many times that morning.

Why was I banned from the table? I wondered, looking at the empty chair. I dared not enter the room. How unwanted I felt. The emotional tone of the conversation was to me like a damp, smelly dishcloth.

Voices were low and controlled, unlike the usual out-of-control tone, in high volumes, its intensity piercing my ears. Calmness grounded everyone around the table that day. My sister Debbie sat across from my gray, stone-faced father. He had moved out of our home twelve months earlier, never once suggesting I go and live with him. Was it guilt I could see in those steely eyes? He cared for the wayward Boys' Brigade boys, teaching them in his office after work, but somehow, I, his second daughter, was too difficult, too much work, or would cost too much. Who knows? I do not recall hearing Dad give an explanation while I eavesdropped on the meeting. It was my sister's voice I heard break through, "We'll have her."

Still burning with curiosity, I recently asked my sister if she recalled what reason Dad gave for not putting his hand up to have me that day. She didn't remember, either. No doubt Dad had his reasons. Too late now. He took them to the grave eleven years ago. Hmmm, what a life lesson right there; do what's difficult and have that conversation.

My dear, for-the-moment-sober mother sat numb and silent beside Debbie. I recall seeing her eyes: red, empty, washed out from the night's tears. Dad was right. My poor mum could barely look after herself, let alone me. She had drunk the night away so many times. Somehow, staying upright on the piano stool, she'd attempt to soothe her pain by playing all her old favorite hymns: "What a Friend we have in Jesus," "The Old Rugged Cross," "Amazing Grace," "How Great Thou Art," "Blessed Assurance," "Guide Me, O Thou Great Redeemer."

I'd drift in and out of sleep, comforted by her beautiful playing. After what felt like hours, I'd throw back my warm blankets, tiptoe out of the bedroom I shared with Debbie to the lounge. Chilled from the night air, gently reaching across the keyboard, I'd put my little hand on Mum's cold, damp hand, feeling the tears drop from her cheeks as she looked up at me. We wouldn't speak. I'd lead her to her empty bed. Long had it been since she'd experienced the love that once came from that bed. Mum's comfort for a loveless marriage and a life of broken dreams was her bottle, her music, and her tears.

I'd tried to block out the sounds of life swirling around me—angry words, crying, physical fighting, and hours of late-night hymn playing. One thing I couldn't erase were the visions—the wooden frame at the end of the keyboard, stained from the empty glasses; the half-empty bottles hidden behind the curtains. I saw my Mum's half-empty life. My mother blocked life out the only way she knew how. Such were our similarities; her life was out of control, and I had no control over mine. I was just a child.

Dad, in stark contrast, filled his life, always on the go and out of the house. He loved his role as Boys' Brigade leader. I learned how much he longed for a boy years later when he remarried. His first child was a boy, Isaac. I recall Dad telling me the name meant "long-awaited son."

"Come on, Dad. You and I both know that isn't true," I said with a broken heart, feeling rejected.

Dad had been in seminary, so I knew he knew the story of Isaac. The name Isaac means 'laughter'.

For the record, God told Abraham that he and his wife Sarah were to have a son and were to call him Isaac. Abraham fell on his face and laughed, while Sarah laughed to herself. Did God not know how old they were (Genesis 17:17) *and* she was barren? I would have had a condescending chuckle, too.

God was true to His word. This is what happened.

> *Now the Lord was gracious to Sarah as He had said, and the Lord did for Sarah what He had promised. Sarah became pregnant and bore a son to Abraham in his old age, at the very time God had promised him.*
> Genesis 21:1-2

In the chapter to follow, you will learn the meaning of my name and the powerful impact that had on my life.

So, anyway, my two parents were victims of that universal truth—change. Their feelings changed for each other. Falling out of love, they could envisage no future together. I was piggy in the middle. Maybe that was why Debbie called me Piglet.

Thankfully, that name didn't stick.

Hearing from the meeting room "We'll have her" changed everything.

No more hearing Mum cry.

No more sleepless nights.

No more arguments and violent acts.

No more heavy door knocks from the police.

No more visits from the telecom technician, reconnecting the phone.

No more running away into the local park.

This was going to be an experience of a lifetime. What a new beginning. I was excited. Did I care why Dad didn't or wouldn't have me? I don't recall giving it one thought. Debbie and her husband Doug had stepped up for me. How generous. What a responsibility to take on, having another's child, a little sister, sharing your home, and what a blessing I'd just received.

"Thank You, Lord, for hearing a little girl's prayer: "*Stop the fighting.*"

I certainly hadn't seen that answer coming. What was next, I did not know, except I was on the move and so grateful.

My future looked bright. Now I laugh. My name was "Carolyn Bright." What's in a name? Well, more than you might think.

Deep down, I was torn by what was, what *could* have been, and my broken family. I longed for harmony. Family unity. "Divorce," a dirty word for me, came to pass. Never would birthdays, Christmas, and holidays be the same. I knew I didn't understand half of what had happened. Leaving my parents in the rubble of their choices, I had a choice to make: Was I going to sink or swim?

What now? captured my thoughts and my focus. I was keen to make the best of all the possibilities: new town, new home, new neighborhood, new school, new friends, new sports teams…everything, in fact.

The wide-open windshield ahead presented a translucent future. No looking in the "fear-view" mirror. I fueled up on the damage of my past. Now, knowing it wasn't my fault, I was moving on. There would always be that question, "Why?" Would even knowing the answer affect anything?

I knew where I had come from, and it was over. No more. I was a kid from a broken home, but I was far from broken. I felt so much stronger. I had survived. No more thuds that rattled my peace and no longer needing to hide under my sheets. The road cleared of debris gave way to a world of opportunity. I would not mess it up. The raw truth of my past was the fuel I needed to fire up and move on.

> The raw truth of my past was the fuel I needed to fire up and move on.

"You survived that poor start, so anything's open to you," I told myself.

How true that would prove to be when I learned the meaning of my name.

Reflection:

How do you handle change?

Are you stuck with the *Why?*

How would your future change if you asked, "What now?"

What damage fuel could you use to move ahead?

3

The Past Has Purpose

I came to learn the important lesson in the chapter title years later. I just needed to find the light switch to see.

Impacted from listening to a Black Lives Matter podcast, I let the insight of a young African American girl sink in. After visiting the Smithsonian National Museum of African American History and Culture (NMAAHC) in Washington, DC, wise beyond her years, she spoke; the gist was that in order to move forward in life, you need to stop and know your past. No hiding what was, no sweeping the tough issues under the rug. Face the realities of the days gone; then write a new future with the knowledge and wisdom of what went before.

Until we stop, face, and heal the wounds of our past, they will continue to bleed, leaving a stain on our lives. Want change? Take the young girl's advice. Stop. Reflect. Ask for help. This can be hard making us profoundly vulnerable. Learning how to ask and when, takes time but is so worth the effort. It is here where you can let go of what you inherited from your past and write your own future. I touch on this further in later chapters.

> Until we stop, face, and heal the wounds of our past, they will continue to bleed, leaving a stain on our lives.

While I was traveling in France, across my path came the same message. Was this a coincidence? I had been visiting the little riverside village of Amboise; here I learned where Leonardo da Vinci (1452–1519) spent the final years of his life. How peaceful. It was a cold November day. The sunlight peeking through the trees reflected soft images on the historic Château du Clos Lucé.

Wandering through his garden, I reflected on how nature inspired his work. Largely self-taught, he found his own answers, weighted heavily in observation:

> Nature is filled with infinite causes that experiments have never demonstrated.
>
> —Leonardo da Vinci

Immersed in the wonderful scene of peace and calmness, I strolled through the spectacular Italian-style Renaissance garden, with its tranquil ponds and meandering pathways to a mysterious woodland. Seeing his work on display took me by surprise, as my limited knowledge only knew him as the painter. How wrong I was. He was Leonardo the engineer, the visionary, the painter, botanist, sculpturer and the architect.

Something caught my eye. As mist rose off the lake with a cool November breeze sweeping through the centuries-old pines and Italian cypress trees, hanging elegantly on the limbs of these glorious trees were translucent canvases, depicting his designs. Each painting was nine to-twelve-feet tall. What a mastermind.

Entering the château, I was invited to walk the past, some eight hundred years. More of his work was on display: manuscripts and notebooks of his drawings and sketches. I was amazed.

Marveling at the creative mind of this man, I continued further. Projected on a wall, Leonardo's quote caught my attention:

"Fear of the dark and the threatening cavern, desire to see what marvels might be hidden within." *Leonardo da Vinci*

Unexpectedly—Leonardo's words drawing me into action, shining the light into the crevasses of my life, forgotten, buried—I felt quite emotional. Was this where life was hiding? As I stood there, fearing the winter of my past, bleak and cold, where everything had died off, the voices of Leonardo and the young girl from Black Lives Matter were ringing in my head, inviting me to explore a hidden world. As the words illuminated a light of desire in my heart, I knew they had gifted me with a key to something new. Beneath the crusty cold and even frozen soil, just maybe, life *was* hiding in the dark.

> *Beneath the crusty cold and even frozen soil, just maybe, life **was** hiding in the dark.*

Interestingly, reading Dan Allender's workbook *To Be Told: Know Your Story. Shape Your Future*, I came upon the same message. This was no accident. Taking the risk, I plunged onto the path. I looked back.

First, behind me, I saw the beauty in the landscape of family: the communion of love, care, belonging, hopes and dreams, support and instruction; the conversations around the dinner table, the laughter, and the joy of unity with those I loved. Then when my shalom shattered, the beauty faded into a distant sunset, where darkness loomed and grew. With each fractious moment, fear, despair, anger, hurt, lies, anguish, and brokenness formed. You know the story now. That bleak season—its arguments, sleepless nights, and police visits—finally gave way to stillness and quiet.

Like a workout I hadn't chosen, the pain gave me purpose. It highlighted the hidden lie I had believed: that I would end up like my parents. I *had* believed that deep in my heart. Stop a moment. Isn't it interesting how you spell "believe"—with *"lie"* in the middle? Now look at how you spell "heart"—*"ear"* in the middle. Who do you listen to and believe? What lies deep in your heart that you believe? Who has stolen your heart and your joy? Do you feel imprisoned and trapped in your past?

The Art of the Essay: From Ordinary Life to Extraordinary Words, by Charity Singleton Craig, highlighted the repeated theme: look back, ponder life—your own life.

I discovered, in wrestling with my past, recreating my life's experiences, stopping to reflect, thinking about it, while putting the shattered broken pieces with all their sharp edges together, there were secrets to uncover. Pieces I didn't know belonged, having been scattered, revealed something new.

As if I were looking down a kaleidoscope, with the broken pieces now clearly seen, my past transformed into a thing of beauty. I turned the tube of memory. The colored pieces of the past were providing a new vision.

My life has been shaped by fragments of truth, love, laughter, loss, fear, discomfort, disappointment, lies, and heartache. As with regressing in time, in the Château du Clos Lucé, I walked through my past, discovering comfort, wisdom, and hope. I'd wanted to bulldoze those painful rooms of memory. Instead of a heap of jagged memories, piled in a heap on top of each other, they had indeed revealed a secret. They had invited me back to:

View with new eyes
Have a bigger heart
Have a clearer, more open mind

Forgive more
Love better

I invite you to do the same. Seeing your past from a different perspective, above the turbulence of your past, changes things.

When you pay close attention, as described in *Bird by Bird: Some Instructions on Writing and Life* by Anne Lamott (in which she calls life "a whisper of essays"), you will discover something miraculous and extraordinary in the everyday.

> When you pay close attention, you will discover something miraculous and extraordinary in the everyday.

Life is truly a gift full of mystery and miracles.

God showed me through Rick Warren's devotional teaching of Daily Hope that knowing my SHAPE—**S**elf, **H**eart/passion, **A**bilities, **P**ersonality, and **E**xperiences—molded who I am. I marveled.

Reflection made me aware that while growing up before my time—being the adult—made me tackle life head on, I was a survivor. My personality, loud and bold, being a risk-taker, had catapulted me into opportunities I was eager to take. All these life experiences developed me. It was my ah-ha moment.

Mum asked me the other day, "So, dear, what have I taught you?"

"Truthfully, Mum"—pausing with hesitation— "how not to live."

Her eyes dimmed with sorrow as I spoke those harsh words. Wrapping my arm around her, I continued, "It has been the most valuable and costly lesson. Sitting on the sidelines of your life, watching your journey through deep troubles and great turbulence—while it truly makes my heart ache, you have shaped my life for the better. I am so grateful while sad all at once. Thank you, Mum. I love you so very much." We both cried.

Reflection:

Where could you discover marvels in your past?

What are ways you could change, knowing your past, to give yourself a better future?

How willing are you to look into the crevasses of your past?

Ask yourself; *Who am I? What am I on this planet to do?*

4

Names Have Meaning

Returning to New Zealand in the summer of November 2018, I visited Mum and stepdad Ceddie. Sitting high on Cashmere Hill, their little home looked out onto spectacular sights over the city of Christchurch. The twilight, shimmering through Mum's living room window, lured me outside. Behind the house was a fabulous path. With my walking shoes on, I began winding my way up the hill towards the summit, "The Sign of the Kiwi." Chirping birds greeted me. Smells from the native trees, swirling around my nostrils, delighted my senses, while the sights that appeared around each corner had my heart skipping. Trying to capture the moment, I snapped away with my iPhone. Then the early evening gave way to the most picturesque sunset; brilliant yellows, oranges, and reds. Lit up by the setting sun, the clouds, like a warm blanket, covered the sky. Christchurch and the countryside far below looked to be resting. Far, far away over the plains, the spectacular snow-capped mountains of the Southern Alps stood tall. Some twelve months earlier, a horrendous fire swept with frightful speed across the hills, terribly scarring everything in its path with intense burning, leaving the landscape bare.

Looking around me, I saw signs of new life—little green shoots sprouting up from the ground and in the charred trees. Lifting my spirits with glorious singing were the native bellbirds, tui, and various other birdlife. I watched tiny little fantails flitting from branch to branch, and tree to tree. What joy. How mysterious is the circle of life!

Back from my evening walk, I was welcomed by Mum's cheerful voice the moment I stepped through the front door. "I've turned your blanket on."

Wonderful. My dear Mum knew exactly what I needed, warmth to wrap around my aching joints.

Having gone through a hip replacement years earlier herself, she understood my pain. With *my* procedure looming, I knew I had to press on with activity—paying attention to the voice of my therapist, which rang in my head: "The joint needs to be nourished with good blood circulation. Walking is helpful."

Turning in for the night, I saw my journal sitting on my bed, titled: *"For I know the plans I have for you," declares the Lord, "plans to prosper you and not to harm you, plans to give you hope and a future."* Jeremiah 29:11 (NIV).

What an appropriate daily reminder. When life throws a curve ball and I am unable to see the woods for the trees, His perspective takes me higher. I considered the fire, caused by a natural phenomenon—lightning. Whilst destructive, scarring the land, it brought positive outcomes. When left in place, dead organic material affects smaller plants and organisms. It stunts growth. Isn't that so true for our lives? When we hang onto the past's "dead organic material," our life *is* stunted.

The "fire" of our lives makes us stronger, like those burned trees. They survived. Cleared of the undergrowth, no longer competing for light, food, and water, they grow stronger. I love the hand of God in nature, in life. He works things for good. I considered the scarred relationships of my past: dismal, hopeless, and

> The "fire" of our lives makes us stronger

so damaging. Flashing into my mind was the vision of the new life I'd seen on the hill, climbing to the summit. That got me thinking. Scaling my mountaintop trials, coming under fire, I'd experienced my own burn-off. Painful and scary, yes. However, fresh growth appeared. There had been a purpose in my pain. I was stronger, with fresh growth and nourishment coming into my life from places I hadn't expected. How interesting and grateful I was for that image.

Having left the workbook in Chicago, I had with me the actual book, *To Be Told: God Invites You to Coauthor Your Future*, by Dan B. Allender, PhD. Reading Chapter 2, "What's Your Real Name?" stopped me in my tracks.

Let's check Mum's name.

Entering *Rosemary* into my phone, thanks to Google, I read on:

> ROSEMARY: from the Latin Rosmarinus, meaning "dew of the sea"; salty texture and ability to thrive
> Symbolizes remembrance…
> Herb: adds fabulous flavor, leaves a beautiful aroma; has a flower that is delicate, fragile, and beautiful

In *Hamlet*, Ophelia passes out herbs and flowers and Laertes says, "There's rosemary; that's for remembrance. Pray, love, and remember."

Reflecting on Mum's life, I'm very aware of the splinters of evidence where she lived into her name; glimpses of beauty interwoven with tragedy. Despite her avalanches of trial and tribulation with a salty texture, she could claim seasons of growth, albeit achieved through great perseverance. Certainly, delicate and fragile, *and* beautiful, she knows how to pray, and she taught me. Oh, my very dear, loving mother.

Mum, always so generous, gave away to friends and neighbors the roses she'd tenderly grown. Always choosing those with the best perfume, she brought love, leaving lasting memories: truly, an aroma of generosity, while the roses emitted their own glorious smell. Now living in a retirement home, playing the piano to the old folks, as she tenderly calls them, she is still leaving that aroma. She gives with the gift of her playing, good cheer, and comfort. Her loving smile is also what you remember, along with those tunes.

"Mum, you are so beautiful."

I was now very curious. What does my name mean? Truthfully, I have never liked it.

People would always say "Caroline" after I had just introduced myself. So annoying. Anyway, Google, do your thing:

CAROLYN
Old German—Free Woman
Italian—STRONG, female name for Charles
English—joy, song of happiness, feminine manly (an alpha female, I'm guessing)

Wow. Never had I reflected on who I was through that lens. How accurate, describing me well—all meanings I gladly claim. *Carolyn* surely is a good name for me. I would never have believed it.

Free Woman: Thinking back, snuggled under my warm blankets, I remember how my parents always encouraged me to try new things. Some might say they pushed me in life. I'd say pushed me into living. I went outside my comfort zone and felt OK out there. Unafraid of the unknown, venturing far and wide. Yes indeed, a *free woman*. Having decided on something, I'd get after it. In my teens, I set my sights on the big smoke—to be a twelve-month international exchange student in Kansas. Maybe not the Big Smoke, but a big move. You can read all about those twelve months in Kansas and other adventures in Part 4 of this book: "Destinations: Let's Go." A free woman, indeed.

Strong: Good at sports, I loved the social and the physical aspect. I was competitive. Dad would take me down to the track to train: 100, 200, 400, 800 meters. I smile, remembering the good days with my dad. I was fit and *strong*.

Years later, living in Chicago, I attended a women's Bible Study Fellowship (BSF). At year's end, the leader placed a little gift on each chair. I chose a random seat and sat, picking up my gift—a little Morse Code bracelet. How interesting. Mine read, "STRONG." OMG! That, my friends, is called a divine appointment. God had planned for me to attend Inco's class that year, be in class that exact day, and sit in that chair. He wanted me to know I was exactly who my parents named me—*strong. Italian male name Charles*—WOW. My dad's second name is CHARLES. A family name. Did he know this when he named me? Sadly, I cannot ask him. With this new knowledge, I had a sense of belonging somehow, despite the fracture of the family. So, some of my manifested genetics, I have Dad to thank for: a love of people, driving, sports, travel, music, the outdoors, and adventure.

Song of Happiness: My song of happiness, for as long as I can remember, is Josh Groban's, "You Raise Me Up." The lyrics draw me out of the dreary playlist in my head. They talk about in times of trouble, weary and feeling down. *If* I choose to sit a while in the presence of God, He will raise me up and enable me to stand on mountains and on the stormy seas of life.

This song transformed my thinking and actions. Having experienced the joy from being raised up, it has encouraged me to be an agent sharing a 'song of happiness' to those around me. I've come to use different forms; a love emoji, a kind word or a verse of hope. Many times, I have received messages back,

"You have no idea how much I needed that right now. Thank you."

I love receiving those little prompts to pause and send a message of encouragement to someone. Like a mirror, as I gave out, so I received back. I felt good.

In future chapters, I talk about the need to pay attention to what you listen to, be aware of what you tell yourself, and how words matter. Being intentional is your ticket to getting out of life's deep valleys.

> Being intentional is your ticket to getting out of life's deep valleys.

Reflection:

Where could you discover marvels in your past?

How could getting to know the real you help you reach new heights?

How would understanding your past give you purpose in the future?

Who could you send a 'song of happiness' to?

Still with me? What I discuss next is knowing what you need for travel. How to journey well through this life of the unknown, change, surprises, and trials.

Part Two

PREPARE FOR THE JOURNEY—TOP TIPS

How great to know we have choices.

How many shoes do I need? What type?

Sandshoes (runners)

Jandals, as we say in New Zealand

Flip-flops, as referred to in America

Thongs, as the Aussies say

Confused? Welcome to the International English Language.

How many pairs of shorts, T-shirts, dresses, jeans, and so on?

Ever been on a holiday with a supersized bag, only to return with clothes and shoes you never wore? My experience and advice: travel light.

5

Travel Light

It's not always *what* you pack that's the problem. Packing *too* much and carrying around excess luggage—*that,* my friends, is the problem. Oh, the weight and cost. I learned the hard way.

In September 2010, living in Australia, I was already thinking ahead to our summer holidays and Christmas back in New Zealand at the Deck family's beach house on Lake Taupo. In our reversal of the seasons, summer is December, January, February. My mind paused, imagining the early peaceful walks around the lake's edge as the sun danced, glittering like diamonds on the surface. The native forest with tui, fantail, and bellbirds singing as they flitted from tree to tree. The early-bird angler trawling the calm waters for breakfast. Freshwater trout. Yum. There is nothing better. Off your fishing rod into a hot pan, lightly seared with a dollop of butter, a slice of lemon, and a pinch of salt and pepper with your first coffee for the day. That all makes for a fabulous Kiwi breakfast.

Just thinking about holidays at the lake had me daydreaming.

Our family bach at Omori was our home away from home and what we *all* longed for; the endless summer days with fishing, skiing, swimming, cricket on the front lawn, BBQs on the deck, reading under the tree, coupled with laughter and singing late into the night. Bring it on!

It was only September, but I'd prepacked my bags with fear and anxiety, dreading criticism from a family member. I'd exhausted myself, losing sleep, recycling the expected conversation like a tape on replay. As I lay on my back, looking at our bedroom ceiling, over and over, it reran each night.

What made it worse, this was a private conversation. I hadn't disclosed my feelings to anyone.

I can hear you asking, "Why didn't you share your worries with your husband?" Filled with pride and fear, I was too embarrassed.

Have you experienced something similar? Wouldn't you agree that it's fear and pride that so often get us stuck?

> Wouldn't you agree that it's fear and pride that so often get us stuck?

Not wanting to lug this baggage around for the next three months, I decided to get help.

I reached out to my pastor.

Lesson 1: Little did I expect that sharing my feelings would set me down onto the path of dumping the load. Asking questions, like kites flying in the wind, got me thinking.

Lesson 2: He had me refocus.

What did I want from that person? *Reply:* I wanted affirmation. I wanted to hear I was doing a good job raising our five children in Australia, away from family and friends, while Brendan, my husband, spent weeks away working.

What will happen when this relative criticizes you, instead? What will hubby do? *Reply*: Nothing. Brendan knew the gentle approach resulted in healthier outcomes.

How does that make you feel? *Reply:* Irritated. Why? Because that was not my nature, and inwardly, I knew he was right.

Tell me about your relative's relationships. Did I know about my critic's childhood? *Reply: Pause.* Hmmm. That took some thinking. Where was Pastor Richard going with these questions?

Does he receive affirmation from the family? *Reply:* Now that you ask, *thank you, you're great, good job* were missing.

Q: So, how can someone give something without first possessing it? *Reply:* Good point.

Lesson 3: Give away what you need and get what you want. This is the "reap what you sow" principle. I redirected my focus *from receiving to giving*. It's like looking in the mirror— give a smile, and you receive a smile.

Living overseas without family support nearby had me exhausted. When Brendan traveled, my days were long, and— lonely at night—I'd collapse into our empty bed. I longed for affirmation.

Over the next three months, when the phone rang, no matter who it was I jumped at the opportunity to talk. "Hey. Thanks for calling."

Life away from our New Zealand home had its ups and downs, and I always found there was something I needed. I'd finish our call, "I just wanted to say thank you for helping me with this. It means a lot, knowing your opinion."

It did. Drawing from the well of another's life opens room for wisdom to be shared and lessons offered.

Lesson 4: Glean from those who have walked ahead. Don't be too proud to ask. Sure. It isn't easy, as it makes us vulnerable. *If* we just choose to reach out, there's knowledge and understanding for the taking. Humility is a hard coat to wear and is countercultural in today's world, but the rewards are many.

WARNING: Be mindful of whose advice you seek. Is it someone credible? What does their life look like? Be discerning. And be open to those whose opinions differ from yours.

Lesson 5: Gratitude. My attitude changed. I became oddly grateful for the life lessons I needed. I had a new heart, enabling me to use the inner ear to hear, disarming the dread.

Guess what happened. After three months, I forgot about my worries, anxiety, and feelings of inadequacy. The giant hairy monster that had taken up residence in my head, capturing my thoughts, no longer had its grip on me while I lay in bed at night. No longer did I replay made-up conversations. The fear (fretting about the effects of an adverse reality) was gone. Plus, I let go of the anger knot in my chest against Brendan. I'd been mad at him, and in releasing my anxious pictures of what might happen removed the tension.

> *Fear (fretting about the effects of an adverse reality)*

Consumed with my interests, I'd focused on thinking and feeling I wasn't good enough, which led me to an even deeper lie: that this imaginary enemy didn't care for or approve of me. Do you see the downward spiral I experienced when listening to the lie driven by fear? Indeed, my wayward thinking was far from the truth.

Another consequence, *had I not dumped my excess baggage*, was jeopardizing the relationships with those I loved and who loved me, my immediate family. How was my bottled-up emotion impacting my kids and other family members? Picture a pebble dropped into the still waters of a pond. The ripple effect starts small, then multiples with far-reaching rings. I talk in a later chapter about the results of gentle words used versus those thrown out in anger.

As a result, for the first time on returning to New Zealand, I didn't come under attack. No agitating comments.

Want to know the best outcome? The newly trod action steps transformed me. Thanks to the gentle questioning from my pastor, which changed my focus away from "#me," I traveled to New Zealand out of the turbulence I'd created in my head. Seeing the big picture helped. Refocused with a new perspective, I learned how to disempower the feelings of victimhood and walk, empowered, to create an outcome of unity, peace and belonging. It is my suggestion that you keep short accounts of your thoughts and feelings, as storing them up only serves to weigh you down.

> Disempower the feelings of being a victim and walk empowered to create an outcome of unity, peace and belonging.

The Bible teaches that gentleness is a softening in our heart that allows for tenderness and acceptance while it grows and deepens relationships. What truth. What a contrast to my previous thinking. How I thought and behaved completely changed the lead-up to and the outcome of my holiday.

Having dumped my prepacked bag of fear and anxiety, I traveled lighter. I got my mojo back, recharged. I'm sure if you had asked my family, they would have told you Mum was less grumpy and snappy. Happy-go-lucky Mum and "Wifie," as dear, sweet Brendan calls me, was back. The ripple effect spread noticeably.

Reflection:

What baggage weighing you down do you need to address and offload?

How, by refocusing, can you empower change?

Whose life can you improve today as you give out to someone the seeds you want to reap for your own life?

6

Take Your Charger and Adapter

When traveling, it's crucial to have your electrical devices ready to use. It's all about being charged.

We all know nothing works if the battery is dead. What's annoying is traveling to a country where the power point is different, and you have the wrong plug.

Travel tip: Did you know plugs differ as you travel the world?

- New Zealand has three-angled prongs
- The UK has three chunky straight prongs
- Europe has two fat round prongs.

On your international trip you need an adapter, for not only is the socket different, but so is the voltage.

Fast forward to 2016. Now living in Chicago, I boarded a plane bound for New Zealand. Hearing the Kiwi accents of our cabin crew ("Kia Ora. Welcome aboard") was like having a big cuddle. I love New Zealand and the reminder I was still a Kiwi girl after twenty-five years away, even if I had lost part of my accent.

For the next sixteen hours, 24A was my resting place. I was ready. Settling into my seat, I plugged my phone into the socket. Having a multi-charging outlet that works for both New Zealand and American devices at your seat is so convenient. Thank you, Air New Zealand. You make travel easy.

On went my headphones. As I surveyed the entertainment-screen menu, I had choices. Which movie would I watch first? I could enjoy one film before dinner, with a lovely smooth pinot noir in hand, and another after my meal. That would take care of approximately four hours. After a yummy dinner—mouth-watering New Zealand lamb, buttered mashed potatoes, and steamed vegetables, and of course, another local pinot—I checked the flight path. Only twelve hours to go. With the cabin lights dimmed, it was time for sleep. From my prepacked sleeping kit, I put in my earplugs and dabbed lavender oil under my nose, taking five big, deep breaths. Lowering my seat back, my eye mask in position, I burrowed into the pillows.

"Good night."

Hours later, I stirred. The smell of breakfast was wafting through the cabin. With my eye mask off, I gently lifted the window shade. The most glorious orangey-red sky welcomed my sleepy eyes. A beautiful new day awaited. I viewed land thousands of feet below, bathing in the South Pacific, Aotearoa—translated from Māori into English: "the land of the long white cloud." I was almost home.

If I'd only taken a dollar for every time I'd heard, "Oh, you're from New Zealand. I so want to go there. I hear it's beautiful."

Beautiful it is. The emerald-green and contrasting dark deep-blue waters surrounding the shores of our small island, as I gazed out from my window seat, looked stunning. The beaches—some with golden sand, others with black stone—provide a surfer's paradise. Plus, serenity in the out-of-the-way bays nestled around the coast.

Mentally, I took a quick "familiarization" tour, as we called it in the travel industry. Across the country, I saw undulating rich green pastures dotted with fluffy white sheep and cattle and cows of various colors. Contrasting the gentle slopes are the rugged mountains formed by the massive fault line running throughout the country, yielding to spectacular views. Among them, the South Island with so many majestic sites; the Remarkables, standing tall above Lake Wakatipu; Mitre Peak, jutting high out of Milford Sound; misty-cloaked fjords carved out of the mountains by former glaciers; Mt. Cook, majestically towering high in the snow-capped Southern Alps. And that's just the start. New Zealand is a traveler's gateway into a world of adventure. Yes, it is beautiful.

"Welcome home," I told myself.

Feeling the bump of the wheels touching down, I switched airplane mode off my phone.

Pressing the side button, I waited—a black screen. Nothing working. It was dead. It couldn't be. I'd had it on charge for the whole sixteen hours. What now? Holding the side button in again, hoping to see the little apple sign, I waited. But nothing.

With the increased beating in my chest, I had no trouble recognizing that panic was setting in. To say I had a massive dependence on my phone was an understatement; it stored my travel itinerary, boarding passes, diary, unmemorized phone numbers, and *so* much more. Even knowing there was no Apple Store in New Zealand, I wasn't about to trust a non-Apple tech dude to my phone. Oh boy. My thoughts were running wild.

Then I remembered why my backpack was so heavy. I had my laptop. That was the answer; I would log in and, thanks to the Cloud, have immediate access to whatever I needed. Deep breaths calmed my racing heart. Relaxing back into my seat, I knew all was not lost. Thank goodness for technology.

That was my ah-ha moment. There was a parallel truth; reaching out to the Cloud *and* G.O.D— Get Out of the Disaster. Both are readily available.

God, however, offers unlimited resources when I tap into His provision, and no device is required, unlike the Cloud. To reach God's power source is only a call or prayer away. Far beyond the dilemma of a dead phone, I've experienced His help in getting me through and out of many more debilitating circumstances. I will tell of some examples in the chapters to follow. I've learned that as I've leaned on human and worldly resources, they disappoint, run out, or simply disappear. On the other hand, God has never disappointed me, is never too busy, silent or inactive and is always present. His Holy Spirit is everywhere, available 24/7. God's personal love and care for His children cannot be overestimated.

This world offers many outlets for powering up. Many, I have tried. But nothing sustainable.

When I grow weary, I can turn to God for He never does.

"But those who hope in the Lord will renew their strength. They will soar on wings like eagles; they will run and not grow weary, they will walk and not be faint." Isaiah 40:31

You know this: life changes constantly. What was current yesterday is not today. This time in history has us experiencing an unprecedented rate of change.

Now, here's the thing. Being the author of my story, I have the authority to tell you from experience that knowing Him as I do, there is nothing more reliable or powerful than God. He never changes. He has been my anchor in the sea of change and is

there is nothing more reliable or powerful than God.

my life's foundation, solid as a rock. Just keep turning the pages to learn more.

My biggest battle has always been the short circuit of my mind. Thankfully, as I've opened my mind to the truth God has shown me, sitting quietly with my open Bible—Basic Instruction Before Leaving Earth—it has rewired my negative thoughts into the truth. He made me for a relationship with Him, to be loved and to love, to know my *true* identity, to overcome, to live free. So what do you think about God? Need help to get you started? In Appendix 2, you will find verses and references that have fundamentally changed the direction and outcomes of my life. From frustration, anxiety, turbulence, and fear, to deliverance receiving peace, comfort, understanding and certain hope. This can be the same for you. Check them out.

> to be loved and to love, to know my **true** identity, to overcome, to live free.

As you keep reading, you will continue to glean practical ways to grow, become refreshed and empowered to move forward.

As if being plugged into a transformer, an almighty power source, the Creator of my being, Almighty God knows exactly how my body works and what I need. Every day I need nourishment physically, emotionally, and spiritually. So, I plug in.

Take writing this book. I won't lie. It has been one of the most challenging tasks I've taken on. Delving into my past has been draining. It's hard looking into those dark chasms where pain and hurt resided. Thankfully, God has walked alongside me, giving me the strength and resources I needed. Such love and gentleness. Receiving new and incredible insight healed my pain and led to restoration—with myself first, then with others—relying on His unlimited power, ever present, for precisely what I need and when.

Just today, as I sat at my desk, my laptop died. The white charging cord lay across my desk, so I plugged it in. After about twenty minutes, the screen was still black. I got on my hands and knees under my desk. There lay the charger, unplugged. I couldn't help but laugh to myself. Yes, I need to stay plugged into the power source.

Reflection:

How does that compare to your life?

Do you find yourself drained and unable to recharge?

Access your charging devices and compare them to God's promises for you.

What's holding you back from asking for His help?

7

Noise-Canceling Headphones and a Great Playlist

How far we have come. From overly large headphones to noise-canceling *small* earbuds. Use them for exercise, even swimming, or take the laid-back option of the couch or your favorite chair. And remember to pack them for that long trip. Great for the plane, they shut out that screaming baby behind you in seat 25A.

But wait a minute. What about the constant everyday playlist we listen to in our minds? Any noise canceling there? With little or no filtration, our minds, as with osmosis, absorb these multimedium messages. Before we know it, they park in our minds, influencing our very being. Is it just me, or are you shocked by where your mind goes and what you think? How at the slightest incident you can get ticked off. I know I am.

Long before now, great thinkers have spoken to this very topic. Here are two examples: "As you think in your heart, so you are"—King Solomon (990–931 BC). Proverbs 23:7

Cogito, ergo sum! ("I think; therefore, I am")—René Descartes (596–650), *Discourse on Method*

Have you ever stopped to consider history through the lens of human minds? What influenced our forefathers? What drove them to act and react as they did? Take the extreme contrast in behavior of Hitler versus Mother Teresa. What motivated them? A factor in the later life of Hitler is that he seethed with resentment and a desire for revenge in response to an arrogant, abusive father: "According to psychoanalyst Michael Stone, Hitler's father reportedly beat both Adolf and his older brother with a whip regularly, meting out daily whippings to the more rebellious Adolf, who, by the time he turned 11, 'refused to give his father the satisfaction of crying, even after 32 lashes.'"[1] By contrast, Mother Teresa was born into a devout family, taught by her mother to care for the ill and the poor. She lived a life of love for all as an expression of love from her father, her Heavenly Father, God.

Taking time to consider this subject of what or who sways your decisions, are you aware of the tremendous powers and influences that surround you? What's your go-to medium? Twitter, Snapchat, Facebook, Instagram, TikTok, Fox News, CNN, ABC, Spotify, Apple Music? What about your favorite playlist? Have you ever stopped to recognize how you feel when you finally switch off? Think about that next time. In our family, we all love Dad's Spotify playlist. It's a rich combination of heavy metal, rock, country, blues, and "cruise and chill." It comes with a touch of Aussie (AC/DC and Midnight Oil); Kiwi (Split Enz, Crowded House, Dave Dobbyn); and many other global bands and artists.

As early as I can remember, our road trips, with five kids in the back seat, had Dad's music pumping through the speakers, everyone singing and moving to the music—such good times. Deck family gatherings most often feature good tunes playing—around the kitchen table, in front of the campfire, or in the car. Thinking of those occasions, I still feel heartfelt emotions—laughter, love, unity, and joy. Special times.

As with the "kite-flying" advice from my pastor, I began to understand the effect words have. It matters who and what we listen to as they influence our behavior.

What can we do? Here are actions I've taken resulting in such positive outcomes.

Air traffic controller:
Notice what is incoming and take control. Send "it" off if negative. Create a NO-FLY ZONE HERE! Don't allow such thoughts and destructive messaging to land.

Change channel:
Refocusing—as I've shared—allows you to change your responses and, consequently, the outcomes.

> Stop and evaluate:
> Is what I hear true?
> Is there a hidden lie in what I be*lie*ve?
> Is what I hear healthy?
> Is what I hear helpful?

If your answer is *no*, go back to the beginning—send it away.

In *Conversations with Myself*, Nelson Mandela conveyed a graphic picture of the dreadful existence he endured, living in his cell at Kroonstad Correctional Center. As the book opens, he shares a letter he wrote to his wife, Winnie Mandela, February 1, 1975, noting how we often judge ourselves critically, concentrating on external factors such as status, achievements, wealth, and our zip code. He challenges us to consider that in an assessment of ourselves, internal factors may be more crucial—what we need is *focus adjustment*, I call it. As Mandela stated, for this we must bring to bear honest introspection.

These issues got me thinking. My cell was my mind. Imprisoned with thoughts and feelings of my past, I *was* stuck. I'd been listening to my playlist far too long; its harmful messaging weighed me down. My emotional remnants kept following me. At times derailed by my thinking, I made destructive choices; they affected me and those around me. I learned, the hard way, we are free to choose, but *never* free from the consequences. I longed for change.

Reading Mandela's book profoundly influenced me. I took a long, hard look at myself. Then the miraculous happened. I flung the door open, pouring shafts of light into my broken and hurting heart, illuminating my past. No longer fearing the darkness, I toured the prison in my mind, slowly opening a door at a time.

> *I flung the door open, pouring shafts of light into my broken and hurting heart, illuminating my past.*

One enormous pain I carried was my dad's death. I could no longer sit with him and listen to his story. No—shut tight was that door, along with many unanswered questions.

Accepting the fact that nothing could change the past, I nevertheless discovered one door accessible. I had a choice to make. Would I enter?

Before me was the opportunity to learn from the pains of yesterday, let go, improve who *I* was, and move on. The ball was in my court and the racket in my hand. Awareness and admission of the past shaped me into the person I am today. Enter, I did.

> *Awareness and admission of the past shaped me into the person I am today.*

STOP…who do you need to talk to before it is too late?

But I couldn't do it alone. You will understand further when you read the chapter "Pastures Green," on destinations.

In the best-selling book of all time, the Bible, we learn that we will be set free through transforming our minds. Free I was. Releasing the weight of sadness, disappointment, and regret was just the beginning.

So again, *stop*. Re-evaluate what you think or believe. Are you living out your life based on something you were once told or are telling yourself? Are you stuck and imprisoned in the past?

In my experience, when plugged into my playlist of choice—the Bible and songs of worship—listening with noise-canceling headphones blocking out my limited and biased views and opinions, I find myself transported to a place of serenity and peace. Tears swell in my eyes like a cup overflowing. It is music to my soul.

Reading the Bible daily, I have learned to *speak* His words into my mind versus listening to the clutter and confusion of my thoughts. Having clarity and truth comforts me and gives me hope.

In my times of greatest need, Get Out of the Dumpster and encounter Greatness Out of Despair; only GOD gave me the keys to unlock my cell. Such is the impact He has. He warns us that there will be trouble and turbulence in this life. He doesn't, however, leave us there. Like the eagle using the storm's force to fly above the raging winds, God promises to give us hope in our hearts as we trust Him, soaring with renewed strength.

> only GOD gave me the keys to unlock my cell.

He promises we will run and not grow weary and walk and not be faint. (Isaiah 40:31) At the end of a tiring day, lying down and grateful for my cozy bed, I listen to His calming words: scriptures of rest where He refreshes my soul and reassures my mind, for surely goodness and love will follow me all the days of my life. It is His playlist I listen to, through which I experience stillness and calm, comfort, and rest. With that said, I go to sleep in peace.

My hope is you will take my example. Press *stop* on your recording, as I did, and start a new playlist that charges your life with hope, strength, and abundant love.

NOTE:
Only a fool repeats his actions multiple times over expecting a different outcome.

BELIEF...ACTIONS...OUTCOMES

My advice is to question your be*lief*. Are you believing a hidden lie?

Reflection:

What are some beliefs from your past that need examining?

What benefits can you find in adjusting your thinking?

Would you be willing to change?

8

Travel Insurance

Yes, you need travel insurance.
Here's a funny story for you.

In 2001 our family embarked on another return trip to New Zealand: five young children—nine, seven, six, four, and not quite two. With four suitcases, a rugby sports bag full of baby clothes, two car seats, a stroller, and a porta-cot, we looked like a traveling circus. As we were waiting in the line to check in for our flight, I overheard a lady behind us say to her husband, "I don't know why they bother."

It was a *lot*, but it was so worth the effort. We had all missed our New Zealand family— fourteen cousins and plenty of aunts and uncles. It was always a blast, going back, as everyone attempted to come together. At the end of an action-packed day, sun-kissed, exhausted kids would fall happily into bed, giving Brendan and me valuable adult time with all the relatives (rellies). Lots of laughter, relaxation, catching up, eating well, and drinking fine New Zealand wine usually led to a sing-along with Uncle Tom on guitar and Uncle Garth on harmonica. Yes, it was worth every effort.

Boarding the plane, I could see the look of terror on the faces of the passengers. I could almost hear their thoughts:

This will be the flight from hell with all those kids. I wanted to reassure them we were ready. Our carry-on bags were filled with coloring books, readers, toys, nappies, wet wipes, bottles, and a change of clothes in case of an emergency. Knowing the pressure in my ears during descent and the need to swallow, I had William's bottle ready, to prevent screaming.

On arrival, we waited for our luggage. Everything slid down the carousel except a sports bag. Brendan, entertaining our three young boys with I Spy—the green bag, the bag trolley—was unaware of my anguish.

Feeling exasperated—pushing Olivia in her stroller, William strapped to my back—I interrupted their game. "There's no sign of the sports bag? It's got all the baby stuff in it."

I was never good at waiting. Thoughts ran wild in my head; sassy, nasty ones, actually, towards whoever took our bag, by mistake or otherwise. *Sucked in! You thought you scored some new sports gear! Too bad. That bag is full of baby clothes. Good luck with that!* How those cutting thoughts took over.

An hour later, the bag still hadn't showed. It never did. I attempted to remember all I had packed for William. I recalled stuffing my new sandals in at the last minute—what a blow.

In that instant, like a lightning bolt, it came to me: from grimace to grin. For the first time, we bought travel insurance. I'll call it the divine nudge. Being New Zealand citizens, it wasn't like we needed health or unexpected accommodation coverage. But we had a lot of luggage, even after I attempted to travel light. After all, we were a party of seven, all ages.

"Just get it, hon," I'd told Brendan. "You never know what may happen." I was grinning. For now, dear sweet William, our fourth boy, would no longer have to wear hand-me-downs. What fun I'd have picking new clothes for him. I loved shopping.

Oh, and I could replace my newly bought sandals.

You may not see it this way, but I saw God's hand over this: Goodness Out of the Disaster. Knowing we would lose the sports bag, He had nudged my thinking the week before, with that little hunch that would not go away: We *would* need travel insurance for that trip.

> My disappointments are His appointments.

I love how God just keeps showing up. My disappointments are His appointments. He was all over it then and promises to be there in my tomorrow. He knows, He sees, and He has the answer.

I *never leave home without Him.* Just as He promised, even out of that bad experience, He brought about good.

God can take you through the mess of life—even the events you brought on yourself—a little beaten up but stronger. His purpose for our pain is to trust Him. He will take us higher than we could ever have imagined; to soar like an eagle with X-ray vision on wings to fly above the turbulence. He will, and He does.

My lifeline insurance verse, *"For I know the plans I have for you,"* declares the Lord, *"plans to prosper you and not to harm you, plans to give you hope and a future,"* Jeremiah 29:11 you can see in action in the next chapter. There is no better insurance than that.

Reflection:

Are you in a mess? Stuck?

Know how to get out?

Call my insurer for help now! He is waiting.

Part Three

PERILS OF TRAVEL

Having spent over forty-five years traveling, I can say from experience that there are pitfalls when it comes to travel. This, you need to know. Some matters, you have no control over; however, some things you can control. Here are just a few I have experienced and learned from.

9

Into the Storm, Seat Belts On

Traveling is not always plain sailing. How unsettling, upsetting, disappointing, and devastating when you get bad news. Take my friend who'd booked her once-in-a lifetime trip to the Antarctic. She had bought extra-warm clothing and a new camera lens, plus planned additional excursions for the cruise.

Then the unexpected happened; a freak wave damaged the ship as it returned from a previous cruise. Her trip got cancelled.

As with my friend's experience, there are always factors outside our control, leaving us unprotected from the consequences.

I got hit by a freak wave I never saw coming, leaving me devastated.

Until that moment, life had presented challenges, but nothing like this. Blindsided and unprepared, I read the email. I was celebrating my fiftieth birthday with family and friends. Lousy timing!

Leading up to my birthday, weeks prior, my sister called from New Zealand, excited to join me. However, I had to put her off. Where would I even be? I couldn't give her a clear answer. It all coincided with rugby.

Our second son, Adam, eighteen years old and in his final year of high school, had been playing the best rugby of his life. His goal was to make his state-representative team and play at the Australian School Boys National Rugby Tournament in Sydney.

This exciting prospect came to a screeching halt. During trials, a player's knees smashed into his back full force, leaving him in excruciating pain. His dreams appeared dashed.

A physio treatment plan required ice bath walks in our outdoor pool—perfect timing, as it was the middle of winter—then hot packs to follow. He then spent hours with the therapist in the clinic. The treatment continued for four days. All the while, I prayed for a miracle. Miraculously, he came good—able to do gentle walking, jogging, and then full speed running.

The players all gathered at the end of the trial week to hear the announcement. Two teams would travel to Sydney. The moment came; he heard his name. Presented with his number-nine playing jumper was his ticket to the nationals. My heart was racing, with tears streaming down my cheeks, overwhelmed with gratitude. God had heard and answered my prayers.

I called my sister, barely able to contain my excitement.

"He made the team. We are off to Sydney tomorrow. See if you can get a flight." Paying with airline miles Award Travel during school holidays was unheard of, not available, and fearing it was too late for even a cheap airfare, I fully expected to hear she couldn't make the trip. However, a single free seat was available. *We will get to celebrate together, after all,* I thought to myself.

Staying with long-term family friends brought a sense of returning home. Over the years, while we lived in Australia, they had been our surrogate family. That I would be there for my birthday seemed so timely. Excitement was building. The week was going to be one to remember.

Then it came like a thunderbolt. It was the morning of my birthday. Deb entered the room, phone in hand—grey-faced, with a look of horror in her eyes. That was not exactly the expression I was expecting. Clearly, I hadn't won the lotto.

"You'd better read this."

Taking her phone and placing my coffee down, I sat at the kitchen table, tamping down my fear, trying to maintain control—my mind racing, for I knew it must have been bad for my sister to react that way.

I don't recall the full content of the email. Just the essential part: "You'll receive a letter of intent from our lawyers, with the outlying of our challenge to Dad's will." Both Dad's younger children signed.

As if a thread were tugged and pulled, in that moment the family unraveled. The betrayal inflicted an immediate, sharp, painful wound.

Angry words exploded from my mouth. Acting purely on impulse, I blurted out, with little restraint: "Deb. How can they be doing this? After all Dad has done and given! Too bad Dad can't talk right now. Wait, he *has* talked. It's called his will. How dare they challenge it? I'm calling."

Deb didn't stop me. We both knew I wasn't one to pussyfoot around, even on my fiftieth birthday. I wanted answers.

I took myself, the phone, and my fury outside, where birds were singing. I could smell the lush green grass and the stunning perfume of the beautiful David Austin roses. However, nothing soothed the turmoil inside me. Nor calmed me down. I needed a response.

The call resolved nothing. Speaking out of anger, I'd lost the opportunity to influence. Proverbs 15:1 (NLT) says that gentle answer deflects anger, but harsh words make tempers flare. Sadly, I was to prove that very truth.

My half-brother and half-sister were undeterred; they were going ahead. "Insufficiently provided for" was their claim.

> *that gentle answer deflects anger, but harsh words make tempers flare.*

Dad would have been heartbroken, I knew. The ripple effect of their decision impacted not just Debbie and me, but many: my children, other family members, and friends. The chain of events that followed were dramatic. To say they sucked was an understatement. They were devastating to our sleep, not to mention to our emotional health, relationships, and happiness. Our shalom was shattered.

For the time being, Deb and I put the news aside—not allowing it to steal our joy or excitement. Not that day, anyway. Bundling ourselves into the car, we headed to the very prestigious grounds of St Ignatius Riverview College.

Admiring the sites on campus as we walked to the rugby fields allowed my mind to wonder. What a challenge, getting here. I was so proud of Adam for pushing through the pain and, no doubt, fear of seeing his dream slip by. Little did I know I would need to call on Adam's admirable attitude of courage, determination, and discipline years later as I faced my own challenges, numerous hip surgeries.

Now here he was, boots on, running proudly out with his teammates onto the field representing Queensland. I felt a small tear trickle down my face.

Then came the big day. After a week of elite competitive rugby, the announcements were to be made; who would be successful and represent their country? A packed auditorium, including players and family, all eagerly waited. Would their son's name be called? It was so nerve-wracking. Alphabetically, the head coach read the list. We didn't have to wait long. "Adam Deck." Losing all control, I stood screeching and clapping. That split-second of delight, pride, and joy had me forgetting myself. Looking around the hall, where hundreds of other kids and parents still expectantly waited, I quickly sat back down, somewhat embarrassed. My heart was skipping, and tears of joy rolled down my cheeks. There was plenty to celebrate. I felt so grateful.

The storm front had hit me hard that week, strewing plenty of damage. Somehow, I needed to get past the unexpected tidal wave that had hit me midships. It took years to work through. I did, nonetheless, having learnt many more life lessons than I'd expected. You'll have to read the outcome in my later chapter "Pastures Green," where I reveal how yet another unforeseen event transpired.

Reflection:

Life is going great one minute, then blind-sided, we are thrown off course. The ripple effects of choices—our own and others'—affect our lives.

How have you responded to the storms of life?

What lessons have you learned?

How have they effected your choices?

10

Flight Diverted

Have you ever experienced this announcement through the speakers: "This is your Capitan speaking. I am sorry to advise that air traffic has diverted our flight because of an unforeseen situation. We will land in forty-five minutes at…"

I'd dropped Fred, our exuberant sixteen-month Bernese Mountain dog, off for seven fun hours with his furry mates at Pupstars Doggie Daycare. My day was clear. I had so much on my list: reading, writing, planning, and studying. *It's going to be awesome.*

Time to myself.

Back home, I turned the key to our apartment, opening the door. That's when it hit me: what happened to *my* day? A laundry bag sat overflowing in the hall. Indignantly walking past, I rounded the corner, only to spy three unmade beds. The massive laundry pile was the hangover from a wonderful visit with my out-of-town kids. Now they'd resumed their private lives.

My husband had been traveling interstate and was soon to be back. "He can't walk into this mess. So much for *my* plans."

Turning to the TV, I hit play for my favorite music on YouTube as I tackled the unwanted laundry and dirty floors; the soothing sounds spread through the room. After I pressed the rotating green light on my Nespresso machine, coffee wafted through my nostrils. It smelt so good—nothing like a hot shot of caffeine to keep me going.

Now, there's a little something you need to know. I struggled to change the bed linen at our place. Freddy, for reasons only known to him, thinks of it as a game. He bounds through the door, leaps three feet out, and lands on the bed. With a circus-type move, rotating, he lands again, this time with paws draping over the edge and his puppy-dog eyes saying, "How cool was that move? Let's play."

So, the next step was to not only slide the bed across the wooden floor back into place after a hundred pounds of flying fur landed but also find the hair-removal gadget. "No, Fred! This is *not* a toy," I cajoled as his puppy mouth, full of sharp, pearly whites, lunged forward, trying to steal the cleaning brush from my hand. More training required do you think? Indeed.

So, with no Fred this day, I removed puppy hair first, stripped the bed down, and threw the sheets in the washer, then later into the dryer. All rooms needed to look lovely and smell sweet before Brendan got home. And yes, the cozy hairballs in each corner of our apartment had to go.

In the background, I could hear my Christian billboard top twenty playing. Listening to worship music is my successful strategy on how to refocus my mind, and slow down. You can look forward to hearing more on slowing down in the Chapter 14: Kilimanjaro: Mountain Climbing

The lyrics hit such a chord with me, reminding me that before I took a breath, God breathed His life into me. When I am lost, feeling alone, and heartbroken, He comes after me, with His never-ending love. He is so kind to me. With a reckless kind of love that never fails. He is prepared to do anything for me, lighting up my shadows so I can see, no longer afraid of the dark and fearful of the oversized issue I imagine. He surely has a reckless love for me.

Having these word penetrate my mind I was overcome with emotion. The tears rolled from my eyes…like a cup overflowing. Even in the space of doing mundane chores, there was always something I could redirect my thoughts to and give thanks for. As my vocal cords got a workout, singing in unison with my favorite artists, Cory, Caleb, and Ryan, secretly fancying myself on stage, I was transformed from *thinking* these words were possible to *believing* them to be true for me.

Wow. I needed that. The past weeks with my boys, who live so far away, were swirling in my mind—the laughter, meals, and fun times. What a blessing, I reflected, to have such a wonderful family. I felt sad to still harbor feelings of resentment looking at my chores while even now, disappointed I couldn't get on to *my* stuff. This is my life, being a wife and mum. It is a privilege. Emotions swelled as a tear dropped off my cheek onto the dirty floor.

Like a dialysis machine cleansing my blood, Jesus's words washed away my ugly, guilty thoughts of begrudging home duties that distracted me from what I'd intended. Now gone, happiness and gratification filled my heart.

> Like a dialysis machine cleansing my blood, Jesus's words washed away my ugly, guilty thoughts

The father of all lies, the Devil, had been messing with me, attacking me on all sides. I could hear his accusing voice, telling me I was so pathetic, getting distracted again; that I'd never get my words out or down. "They weren't worth reading, anyway," the diatribe went on. *Why did I think I had anything meaningful to say? Who did I think I was?*

"You're just good for laundry and housework."

I then heard a gentle, quiet voice say, "The lyrics of those songs are all My words for you. Rest in them. As you do the laundry, make the beds, sweep the floor of dog hair, and get your home ready for your husband, you are following Me. As I came to serve, so too did you. I see you. I know your heart. It is good. You are making a beautiful home for the man you love and being a wonderful wife."

Having made the beds, I noticed a very forsaken-looking yucca tree in a dark corner of my son's room. The soil had dried out finally, after a month of wet feet. I'd almost drowned the poor thing. Dragging it across the room, I moved this miserable plant beside the window to get light. Remembering the Miracle Food (I hoped the name on the box was no exaggeration) in the sink cupboard, I mixed it with water, poured it into the pot, then picked off the dead leaves.

God, as my gardener, reminded me of this exact message in John's gospel. Even when drowning in my life's worries, hiding in the darkness of my thoughts, sidelined by the necessity and impatience to get on, God cuts off every dead branch that bears no fruit.

Every branch that bears fruit, He prunes. He feeds me His "Miracle food," lovingly inviting me into His light, a relationship with His son, Jesus, who is the light of the world.

What a reminder.

Do you miss the blessings, being too busy with the schedule you wrote, seeing the housework as a curse, exhausted by trying to keep your house in shape *and* please your husband? Anxious to complete your to-do list? Feeling shame or guilt because you haven't? It dawned on me: *God had just done a gardening job on me.*

My thoughts transformed. I saw all I had done not as a curse, stealing my time, but as a blessing. I was so grateful:

- that He'd captured my destructive, negative thoughts

- that He'd pruned away my resentment of being Sadie the cleaning-lady
- that I had my loving, hard-working husband, who generously provides
- that my children wanted to be in my life

I was also so grateful:

- for a beautiful apartment high in the sky
- for seeing the breaking of each new day outside our huge windows
- for Freddy's tail-wagging love (not his hair), comfort, and joy

Today I'd experienced proof of receiving more than I'd expected by "serving" with gratitude. Into the bargain, the day was not yet over. Ninety minutes remained of *my time.* I could still write before collecting "little bear." Exhausted from playing with all his furry friends, sprawled out like a doorstop for the next two hours, back at home, Fred allowed me more time to hit my list. I still had four blessed hours before Brendan walked through the door, welcomed by the smell of Pine-o-clean and hot chicken curry soup.

> Today I'd experienced proof of receiving more than I'd expected by "serving" with gratitude.

The big hug and his smiling face would be all the signs of gratitude I needed. It's crazy how when I thought time was against me, God extended my day. That diversion became my payment. I'd take a diverted flight any day if it meant leaving behind frustration and resentment and landing on gratitude and thanksgiving.

Reflection:

What do you succumb to when under pressure?

How could you divert your self-defeating thoughts to re-energize, increase your happiness and good health?

Think what you are missing holding onto your frustration and anger.

11

Trapped at the Airport

Brendan was attending a work conference at beautiful Hilton Head, South Carolina. He was keen for me to enjoy the experience too and asked me to join him before heading back to Chicago.

Twenty-eight tiring hours ago, I'd said goodbye to Mum in New Zealand. Now, after logging all those hours in three different-sized planes in two countries, nearly there, I eagerly awaited the next flight.

Sadly, for me, my day got a lot longer. Black clouds swirled overhead. Violent lightning shafts lit up the sky. Claps of thunder cracked above the voices of the growing numbers of frustrated passengers facing cancelations. Pandemonium broke out. There I sat, trapped at an airport. Where was I, again? It had been a long day. I was exhausted from my long journey, and now the havoc that swirled around me. I longed to see Brendan and the comfort of a cozy bed with crisp, clean sheets.

Ever consider our minds like an airport? With different aircraft on different flight paths, all intending to land—the small private jet, the cargo plane, the regional plane, and the enormous international aircraft. Consider the media flying the airways of our mind. What do we listen to, watch, and read? Many social-media platforms, billboards, TV programs, movies, the theater, magazines, and books scream to get our attention. It gets so congested. What are the conversations we hold with ourselves? Here's the question: ever feel trapped in these thoughts and messages?

I've shared my own experiences, being trapped in the chaos of my mind. When I'm under pressure, it can feel like a state of emergency—too many voices, or maybe just one masquerading as many. I've allowed unwanted thoughts to land, unwanted passengers and cargo to use my head for their destination.

Mind management is a challenge I'm still learning to master. In the last chapter I said music was a successful strategy I've used to redirect my thoughts, but what if that isn't available? Answer. Intentional awareness. I'm working on what lands and what doesn't.

Intentional awareness. I'm working on what lands and what doesn't. I send stuff away.

I send stuff away. *Not going to listen to you!*

This week, being invited onto my author friend's podcast, I talked with her about life. Among her many questions, she asked: How I grew up. How I coped with change. What changes did I make to experience a better way? To sum up what I told her, "Give yourself a P. A. T. each day. Goodness knows we need it."

What is the **P**romise?

What is the **A**ction I would take based on this promise?

What is the **T**ruth I need to know?

Here was my PAT that day:

> P - Multiple blessings flow from gratefulness (Ephesians 3:17–20)
> A - Practice being grateful (Psalm 100:4–5)
> T - All good things come from our unchanging Father (James 1:17)

Looking into my Bible, the authority of truth in my life, I received great comfort and application from these verses that day.

1. Want Blessings?...Yes!
2. Be grateful; make a morning list; start with the right mindset
3. Know God is a good Father, and while this world changes, He never will.

> God has talked truth into my life, allowing me to overcome the lying trap.

God has talked truth into my life, allowing me to overcome the lying trap. When asking, *who am I,* I am His child and *greatly* loved. Philippians 2:13 says that God is working in me. *Energós* is "active, effective, at work." Knowing God has limitless power, I no longer rely on myself. He drove out many fears, worries, doubts, and other self-destructive lies that kept me trapped. His promises set me free. When I trust Him, He faithfully guides me through my day and will continue to throughout my life.

Knowing the Lord as my good shepherd changed my perspective. He has me flying above the turbulence of change. He's told me to pack gratitude, leaving behind bitterness and resentment, for He knows that other flight path: destruction, despair, and depression. What a pilot.

Reflection:

What certain truth are you holding on to? Does it provide a positive application and promise?

What was your experience of being trapped?

If still stuck, what is stopping you from asking Jesus to un-trap you?

12

Pickpocket Thief

We have all experienced losing something. I can get frustrated and even angry by the incredible inconvenience of misplacing my phone.

How about when traveling?

I had a near miss in Lisbon, Portugal. Brendan and I, starving after hours of exploring, strolled past some high-end stores before dinner. Three ladies and a child had stopped to gaze at the overpriced, glittering jewelry. I had my drawstring backpack stuffed with a jacket, passports, wallet, and mandatory make-up purse. We casually smiled and walked by. Unknown to me, those ladies immediately followed us, attempting to get into my bag. As they tried their hardest, I'd felt nothing—no tug on the pack or even that feeling of "You're in my space." But Brendan's brawny arm, now around my shoulders, half pushed me around a corner.

"What are you doing? The restaurant isn't down here."

In his wisdom and experience, Brendan sensed those ladies had been loitering for no good reason and *were too close behind us.* As we walked on, past an outdoor bar, a wide-awake patron called out, "Hey! You might want to close your bag." We stopped in our tracks. As I swung the bag off my shoulder, we discovered it was open. What the heck? Brendan was right with his hunch. Nervously, I dug into my bag, fearing the worst. Thank goodness—all was still there.

"You really shouldn't travel with that easy-access bag on your back. You're asking for trouble."

I felt scolded. However, Brendan was right. It filled me with gratitude to know nothing was missing. The thought of applying for a new passport in Portugal was almost beyond my endurance. It's not what you sign up for on a vacation. I'd narrowly escaped the pickpocket but experienced a loss of safety and security, now feeling nervous.

Constantly stolen in our world is peace. This morning, exiting my building, I walked into a large police presence, lights flashing, and a big black SUV, half on the footpath, rammed between a fire hydrant and a lamp post. A car-jacking attempt bungled. Just my good luck, I'd misplaced my keys, delaying my walk. The police apprehended the offender with no one hurt. Just a smashed-up car. Or so I thought.

My phone was going off. Friends from the building were sending out wild messages. It escalated from video footage and commentary on what happened to another incident the week before, when an evicted resident pulled a gun to footage of a shooting outside a friend's apartment in the next neighborhood over. Within ten minutes, everyone's peaceful Monday morning, the sun shining and birds singing, stolen! There is a thief in our midst. Check out his names: the Devil, Satan, Prince of Darkness, the accuser, destroyer of peace, the evil one, and so on.

From that point on, the temptation was strong to live in absolute fear. Incidents like this were happening more frequently and too close to home. *Thankfully, being the great air traffic controller I am, I stopped that thought in its track.*

That was not the case for the others on the group chat. As they recounted their fears, it was like a fast-growing virus, sending my phone into near overload—showing how all too

shouting, you'll still be on your feet. Truth, righteousness, peace, faith, and salvation are more than words. Learn how to apply them. You'll need them throughout your life. God's Word is an indispensable weapon. In the same way, prayer is essential in this ongoing warfare. Pray hard and long. Pray for your brothers and sisters. Keep your eyes open.

Keep each other's spirits up so that no one falls behind or drops out. Ephesians 6:12– 18 (The Message)

I have not personally counted the multiple times God states in the Bible to "fear not"; however, often enough (I heard as many as 365 times) for me to take notice. So, I need not fear the thief. I suggest you read the last chapter of God's book. It ends well for those who trust Him. That is where my hope lies. An 1873 hymn by Horatio G. Spafford states: "It is well, it is well with my soul." How about you?

Reflection:

How have you experienced the thief, tempter, and accuser?

Where do you look for security in this broken, troubled world?

What have you learned about finding peace?

Part Four

DESTINATIONS—LET'S GO

As a travel agent, I would always ask my client, "What's the purpose of your trip? A holiday *or* to travel?"

I'd get a blank look. Most clients didn't know there was a difference.

Let me explain. A holiday, by my definition, requires spending long, lazy days relaxing by the pool, piña colada in one hand and a good book in the other; the greatest exertion for the day—pushing oneself out of the lounge chair and slipping into the tranquil waters of a glistening pool.

On the other hand, traveling involves a journey full of adventure, packing your best walking shoes for hours of exploring—cities, villages, and sleepy little towns, and taking in as many sights, tastes, and experiences as possible. Travelers find themselves on and off buses, planes, trains, not to mention—in some of my travel experiences—donkeys, boats, horses, jeeps, trucks, and bikes.

Life *is* full of adventure—a constant journey. The words of Pistol in Shakespeare's *The Merry Wives of Windsor* ring true: "Why then the world's mine oyster, which I with sword will open." And while challenging—like prizing open an oyster—if we keep at it, it may unexpectedly reward us.

For some, the thought of an oyster has your mouth watering. For others, it is the menu's least-appetizing item: a wet, salty, plump, chewy oyster. No thanks. I liken it to arriving at an undesired destination.

But what if you discover a highly valuable, lustrous, iridescent pearl? Now do I have your attention?

Understanding how to cope with unexpected situations is paramount, in addition to having the right tools. Have you ever tried to shuck an oyster with a regular knife, screwdriver, or letter opener? Don't be tempted!

Yes, one *big* adventure—that is life. We find ourselves in situations and places we didn't see coming. How do we respond? How well do we cope? Or do we cope?

In the following pages, I will share some of my journeys, all resulting in valuable life lessons.

13

Winfield, Kansas?

In 1979, when I lived with my sister, attending Palmerston North Girls High School, an organization called AFS—the American Field Scholarship—sponsored a seminar for the senior students. Curious and excited by the prospect of world travel, I went. Following a family discussion, I applied to be an exchange student, in whatever spot in the United States they had availability. Much to my shock, I received a letter for an initial interview. I talked my way through the process, realizing it wouldn't be my grades that got me a ticket.

Looking back, I clearly remember this question, presented by the panel of stonefaced, educated-looking people, as I sat in my solitary chair. All eyes were on me.

"What would be your response if your new friends invited you to party, with the likelihood of there being drinking, smoking, and drugs?" (Instant expulsion if caught.)

Without hesitation.

"Well, of course, I would say *no*! If that ruled me out as being their friend, then they were truly not friends for me."

Great answer, I told myself.

Had that reply been enough to get me a seat on a plane and an adventure of a lifetime? Was there a family across the world who wanted a young Kiwi student? That I didn't know.

In my wait, life continued. I was back on the move. Returning to my hometown, Wellington, I found my living environment one I hadn't expected, as by now my family home had been sold. Mum had moved to her newly inherited home in Christchurch, and I moved in with my dad's girlfriend. She was a university student herself. Being young, I didn't question the arrangements. Dad provided for us both.

The challenges of new surroundings, a new homelife, and a world of new friends to make had become my life. I was mastering change, and my new roommate became like another big sister. Life was cruising along better than I had expected; well, that was until I crashed Dad's little sports car. But I won't go there.

I recall the day my life took another turn. The warm summer's afternoon had entered my little bedroom; the massive tree outside my window danced its shadow on my wall, and the birds resting on its branches were singing. I sat on my bed, schoolbooks strewn everywhere. I was a messy, disorganized student. Then, with a grin as wide as the Nile, I saw Dad enter the room. As he held out the large yellow envelope, I saw my name in bold letters—AFS stamped in the left corner. My heart skipped a beat.

Throwing my legs over the side of the bed and kicking away my shoes and socks, I leaned forward to receive the packet.

Dad joined me silently on the bed. I unstuck the tape and, with excited expectation, removed the documents. There were many. As I turned them over, looking at the front page, my eyes gazed straight at the Bowling family: Mum and Dad and two gorgeous girls. Their eyes and smiles beamed with love. They stood on their front lawn under an enormous willow tree in front of their *big* limestone, brown roof-tiled home. *Wow!*

Who are these people who put their hand up to have me for twelve months? I thought to myself.

As if the champagne bottle had blown its cork, tears flooded my eyes and spilled down my cheeks.

I looked across at my dad. Holding hands, we cried together.

We didn't get too far on the first page. Their address read: Winfield, Kansas, USA. Breaking the silence, I blurted out, "OK. So, where in the heck is Winfield, Kansas? Dad, do you know?"

"No idea."

We dusted off the atlas found under a pile of books stacked in the bookcase.

Finding America was easy, with Kansas bang in the middle, but where in the heck was Winfield? Turning more pages, we found the cities page: Kansas City, Lawrence, Topeka, Wichita, and then a barely visible speck, *Winfield*. That would be my home for twelve months.

Fast forward to August 1980. I boarded my first international flight, from Auckland to Los Angeles. I stayed four days at UCLA for the AFS orientation. One afternoon I wandered down to the basketball stadium, seeing players I thought were giants.

Everything looked *so* big. Later that week, I flew to Kansas City, where I met Serge from Belgium and Junko from Japan, my new AFS schoolmates. The three of us could barely communicate; Junko could only say hello, while Serge, with luck, managed an audible English sentence.

It was wild; we spent three hours at a Greyhound bus depot in the early morning, waiting to board our bus to Wichita. I remember a family camping out in a tent pitched between the seats. Our bus couldn't have come soon enough.

Crammed into a full Greyhound coach, we arrived some four hours later. The temperature that hit my lungs as I exited the bus, I thought you'd only experience in the desert. I could hardly breathe the thick air and sweat ran down my back within seconds.

Wearing a black dress sewn by me, hoping for a good first impression, didn't help.

The moment came to meet my Bowling Family. In the bus terminal, welcome banners displayed my name on them. I felt special.

Lori, my big sister, stood next to Betty and Lowell—Mom and Dad. I'd read she had been a cheerleader *and* homecoming queen. Funny, I thought that was just in the movies. Beside her was gorgeous Kim, with a beaming smile. Arms outstretched, she ran to me. She was my age, and we would both be seniors that year. We spent every day together for the next twelve months. How lucky I was.

Little Betty was *so* little. She shone love. Tall Lowell was the gentle giant. After all the excitement, hugs, and bags loaded, we climbed into Dad's *big* gold Buick. What a car. What a ride. It was a far cry from our two-door baby-blue Triumph Herald. I'd never sat in such a luxury car, with its soft, sweet-smelling leather seats, before. Thank goodness we could close the window and turn on the air conditioning. That was a first. Our little car only had the natural kind; window down, wind blowing your hair across your face.

Going to school in Midwest, USA, was a surreal experience for this Kiwi kid. The boys were real cowboys, chewing and spitting tobacco, sporting cowboy hats, boots, and buckles and driving their pickup trucks to the largest student car park I'd ever seen.

I felt I'd landed on a Hollywood movie set.

Besides the laughs erupting as students and teachers tried to understand my Kiwi English *and* the terrible mistake I made of asking a school jock for his rubber, meaning his eraser, life in Winfield was great fun. We spent the hot summer nights at the baseball diamond with classmates, and during winter, families and the entire school turned up to cheer on our football team.

One of the most exciting opportunities came when Bob, Lori's boyfriend, invited me to his basketball game. His dad flew me in his plane to their interstate match against Oklahoma. That was beyond crazy.

Now, life wasn't always plain sailing. For Mom, I added to the grey hairs hiding under that brown color. The night I got home two hours after curfew was terrible. The locked doors had me banging on the back door. What was I thinking? After many a night getting home before midnight—house rules— somehow, she'd heard I'd been riding in a car with boys. Yes, that was true. Technically, anyway. They were the brother of my AFS friend Serge, along with Serge's buddies. *No harm there; One girl and a bunch of guys(!)* I thought. With this dastardly deed I managed to get on the wrong side of Mom, again. I'd become frustrated.

So, on that one evening, after trying to do right, getting home before the curfew, I turned rebel. With no mobile phone to tell anyone of my whereabouts, I got home at 2am. Selfishly, I admit.

As with all decisions, (especially poor ones), there were consequences. I called it the silent treatment. Yes, there was tension in the air. I'd brought unrest into this peaceful family. Stubbornly, that next week, I'd retreat to my room after school and meals. I enjoyed my company, listening to music, writing letters, and hanging out alone.

> As with all decisions, (especially poor ones), there were consequences.

Besides, I felt it was best to keep a distance from everyone until the tension disappeared. The problem was, it didn't go away, affecting my relationship with the entire family.

Swelling up in my mind were memories of my younger years in a turbulent home. It made me sad. But this time was different; *I'd* caused the tension. Growing up, I'd rarely heard anyone apologize—just more angry words—so I knew an apology would be difficult, but I also knew I needed to make it.

I pulled myself together and nervously headed out of my room. Delicious aromas were wafting up the stairs. I found Mom in the kitchen. Facing my fears, I'd experienced that the thoughts held in my head were worse than the reality. With humility, I admitted being in the wrong and said sorry.

> *so I knew an apology would be difficult, but I also knew I needed to make it.*

(For the record, it doesn't count if we say "sorry, but…").

Gracious and forgiving, Mom wrapped her little arms around my body.

"I can't imagine living in a foreign country, away from my family and friends. But, hon. We love you and were worried. Next time, please come home at our agreed time."

My selfish actions had been thoughtless. I shed a little tear. Mom might be little in stature, but she gently taught me a big lesson. *Respect.*

Reaching up, she took hold of my face, looked deep into my eyes, and said three beautiful words, "I love you."

Later that evening, I apologized to the whole family for selfishly planting the seeds for the unpleasant environment. It felt so good to say sorry, releasing the heavy guilt I'd been lugging around. We could now move on.

My twelve months with the Bowling family showed me what a loving family looked like; how they spoke to each other, listened, encouraged one another—and the sweetest of all: each night, I heard them say, "I love you."

1980–'81, my senior year in Winfield, Kansas, was the most positively impactful year of my eighteen years. I had learned what love in action *looked* like: a family willing to take an international student into their home for twelve months. I had also *experienced* love in action: Mom and the rest of the family's forgiveness towards my selfishness. And I *heard* love in action: every night, ringing throughout our home, *"love you."*

Little did I know my unknown destination ("Where in the heck is Winfield, Kansas?") would become a theme in my life—travel. Stepping on that plane and into the unknown was the best thing I could have done. Embracing uncertainty with its challenges allowed me to realize I have choices. Mistakes were merely opportunities to make things right—start over. I transformed my fear into courage by taking action. So, I now encourage you—walk on.

> *I transformed my fear into courage by taking action.*

Reflection:

If you aren't much of a risk-taker, what are you afraid of?

Empower yourself making fear, courage in action.

Consider how your life could change if you practiced humility by saying sorry.

14

Kilimanjaro: Mountain Climbing

No matter how good an athlete—or not—we are, we all entered this world the same: babies, vulnerable, lying around, while others did everything for us. Then we learned to take small steps as we advance through life.

In September 1989, I began another adventure—this time aboard a truck, journeying overland from Nairobi, Tanzania to Harare, Zimbabwe. As a small child, sitting for hours beside the crackling fire, turning the pages of my wildlife books, I'd fallen in love with the wild animals roaming free across the African plains. The shaggy-maned muscular male lion lay in majesty and authority with his pride in the golden savanna grasses, all the while eyes and ears alert; the grace and elegance of a giraffe with towering legs gliding across the plains; the stealth of a hungry cheetah with its long muscular body and legs built for speed, the contrasting stripes of the zebra, the enormous presence of an elephant, gentle yet intimidating. And so many more.

I'd dreamed of this day.

Testing the reality of my dream as I approached the truck to meet my fellow travelers, I literally pinched myself. Yes! I *am* in Africa. Nerves of excitement lifted me into the truck. This was going to be wild.

Like any good travel agent, I'd done the research, and Dragoman Overland Tours was to be my family for the next *twelve weeks*. I put my trust in their sturdy, iconic orange-and-white Mercedes-Benz® trucks, ours named Tallulah, with parts readily available throughout Africa. If we broke down—highly probable given the copious hours on corrugated, unsealed roads and tracks ahead where a lot can go wrong—it was critical that Dragoman could acquire parts. The trucks are customized with an integrated cab to allow engaging with your driver at any time. And there's comfortable coach-style seating, which, believe me, you are so grateful for. These trucks are fully equipped for self-sufficient wild camping, having large, fully opening windows to let your camera take that perfect snap. Their drivers, trained mechanics, are often called to work into the night after long hours of driving. This, we witnessed many times. They are awesome. Just as important was their training on border crossings, which can be difficult due to language barriers and even black-money bribes to officials. A bottle of scotch was always tucked under the driver's seat, I came to learn, for such an occasion. This trip was not for the faint-hearted. But then, I thrived in such adventures: changing schools in my teens; being an international exchange student; experiencing new countries and different cultures when working as a travel agent. Yes. Adventure was in my blood. As for showers and toilets, *scarce* is all I'll say. Sleeping under the stars, in awe of the majestic night sky, transported me back to my childhood— my tent pitched at the top of Poppa Bright's property. Seeing the animated photos from my books—the roaming lion prides, elephant herds, water buffalo, gazelle, and giraffes freely grazing on the savannas—left me powering through my rolls of film. Smitten by the glorious views through my lens, I was in real fear of running out of precious film. Digital wasn't a thing back then. *Slow down, Carolyn*, I told myself.

Stopping randomly in the middle of nowhere at the end of each long day always yielded a surprise. It wasn't *nowhere* for the little faces we encountered as we collected wood for our evening fire—these savanna plains were their home. The joy on their faces as they greeted us was all we needed to feel welcome. I'm not sure who was more excited. The sheer delight oozing from these children melted my heart. Communicating as best we could with hand gestures and much laughter made me realize the power of our humanness. Then came the much-anticipated excursion to climb the majestic snow-capped Mount Kilimanjaro. Yes, that had long been on my bucket list. The tallest mountain in Africa, located in Tanzania, Kilimanjaro, is 19,341 feet to the top. She's clearly viewed, as we experienced, from the rich, nutritious grass plains of the Ngorongoro Crater. As a side note, this is where you can witness the Great Migration, where over two million animals—wildebeest, gazelle, and zebra— migrate from the Serengeti (Tanzania) to the Masai Mara (Kenya) and back. They are faced with the challenge of daily survival, crossing crocodile-invested rivers; hunted by predators and potentially faced with droughts or flooding, depending on the year. Witnessing this migration is truly a natural wonder.

Kilimanjaro, besides the wildlife, is renowned for the unusual terrain, from farmlands, rainforest, moorlands, and alpine desert to the snow-capped summit. That's just for starters. Killi, as she is fondly called by tourists, certainly is a mountain to behold.

In the village at the base is a tourist-information center, where we had the privilege of hearing from a retired walking guide, none other than Miss Daisy. Her face, gentle and somewhat weather worn, suggested a lifetime spent in the equatorial climate with her community of family and friends at the base of her beloved mountain. Her snow-white hair softly drawn back into a bun, she had the gift of her eighty-six years and the wisdom of a well-walked life. Though retired from guiding, she was not done passing on her knowledge. Small in height yet strong, leaning against her carved cane, she spoke passionately yet quietly in "royal" (posh) English, slowly, with perfect enunciation: "Pole, pole [Swahili, pronounced po-lay, po-lay.] You must take it slowly, slowly, slowly. One step at a time will have you reach your goal—the summit." Ringing in my ears was my mother's voice: "You don't have to be like a bull at a gate!" Growing up on a farm, Mum had many times witnessed her father's red-polled Hereford prize bulls, eyes of steel and 1,800 pounds of muscle, heading for the pasture gate. No wonder she had recognized this trait in me. I'd often spoken without real thought or consideration, rushing headlong into things—too quickly and hastily. Fearlessly, I'd grab life by its horns. I was up for this new challenge. Slow would allow me to observe *and* take extra photos. It was so much more than that, however.

> One step at a time will have you reach your goal—the summit.

My lungs burned as the air thinned, the higher up the mountain we climbed. Passing a pile of stones with a makeshift cross at its base shook me into understanding. I had had no idea it truly was a life-and-death reality. Miss Daisy was right. I must pole, pole.

Lungs continually burning for oxygen, and arms, legs, and every other part of my body aching from the final ascent, which incidentally started just after midnight, I made it to the roof of Africa. As the curtain of the night was pulled back by the morning twilight, what lay before my eyes was beyond amazing. There was a sea of cloud; then slowly it parted too, giving way far below to the African savanna. Totally exhilarated,

I felt my exhaustion fade like the night sky. With high-fives and a quick photo session, it was a fast turn-around. As we faced the extreme cold and high winds at the summit, coupled with lack of oxygen, our day was far from over. We had a long way to descend, back down the rocks and scree (loose stones) to camp. All in all, it had been the most tiring, draining, fatigue-creating, extreme eleven hours of my life.

This elation, however, had not been everyone's experience. One of the overland truck drivers, Chris, excited to climb Killi for the first time, had been overconfident, having done army training. Plus, he joked, stubbing out a cigarette, "I smoke, so lack of oxygen is nothing new for my lungs."

Unable to continue due to severe altitude sickness, he needed one of our guides to turn into lifesaver, keeping him warm so as not to die from hypothermia.

Disappointment was an understatement. That had been his "final opportunity to take up a real job"—his words— "before returning to England."

Such is the mantra of this stunning mountain. While Kilimanjaro is an extinct volcanic massif— its last major eruption was 360,000 years ago—the life-saving words of the Swahili people live on.

What a health tonic "pole, pole" could be for the fast-paced, anxious society we live in. Just imagine slowing down and getting connected.

Taking one step at a time, little by little, not racing ahead, we were better able to make considered choices versus rash, instinctive decisions. What a great way to reach our goals. With a slower approach, we got to observe all that surrounded and opened the door to connection—and to the possibility of supporting each other in the journey.

It is, however—in our crazy, 24/7 hectic life—an intentional choice, unlike my Mt. Kilimanjaro experience, *which forces you to slow down.* Tethered to our computers, phones, and Apple watches, we're connected better than ever, albeit through a device. We even expect cafés to provide free Wi-Fi. Next time you are out, see if I'm right.

It got me thinking: *What am I dead to, being so busy, rushing around ticking the boxes? What am I missing, moving with such haste through life? For what? To accumulate for old age, only to find myself sick as a dog, or worse? Pole pole will get us one way or the other!* Maybe we would do well to adopt the Tanzanian way— "no hurry in Africa!"

But just maybe, as we stop to smell the roses, we notice the things in life that *really* matter and give us joy; we start to appreciate all we *do have* and stop striving for outcomes and possessions that only bring with them more anxiety or momentary pleasure.

> start to appreciate
> all we **do have**

Listening to a podcast on achieving change, I heard this statement: "when the existing pain is worse than the pain of change, *then* you will start." Ouch. You may need to read that again. An ambition without steps is merely a dream. Making it a reality comes with small incremental actions forward, one foot in front of the other, intentionally focused on the goal.

Reflection:

What would improve in your life if you were to slow down?

Who close to you are you missing out on?

Yes or No—do you realize you yourself set your schedule?

After reading this chapter, how will you modify your life pace?

What's your goal?

15

The Deserted Island

Have you ever found yourself on a deserted island? Wondered how you even got there? Felt alone, forgotten, abandoned, anxious, with no way to get off?

As I've reflected on some of my broken experiences, when I felt exactly as I've just said, this was one of my saddest: stuck on a deserted island of tremendous grief. I wanted to share it, for it concludes with an unexpected, miraculous gift of comfort, hope, and love.

We pick up when I was living in Adelaide (7 years) with my husband and five young children. Allowing the sun's warmth to comfort me, I glanced around at my familiar surroundings. I loved my home in Adelaide: the large crepe myrtle tree with its fallen, wrinkled, pastel-pink flowers dusting the deck; the glorious aroma from the wisteria, twisted and clinging to the balustrade; and the kookaburra sitting high in the gumtree. But sadly, they did not soothe the ache in my heart.

Replaying the events of the weekend spent back in New Zealand celebrating a special birthday, I was grieved and heartbroken. I loved my family dearly; however, witnessing their conflicts had me spiraling back into my broken, troubled, heart-wrenching past. Swimming in a rip of emotions landed me on a deserted island—alone in my thoughts.

Don't get me wrong. I was enormously thankful for trips back to my birthplace, New Zealand. Some years, all seven of us returned, while other times, I'd go alone. Our phone calls kept us connected, but nothing beat's being there in person. I loved feeling the tight hugs from my mother's now-frail arms; the happiness Deb and I shared as we soaked in her hot spa, laughing and sipping chilled white wine; feeling at peace as I gazed out at the panoramic views of Canterbury, with its patchwork-colored plains, the snow-capped mountains of the Southern Alps, then out to the east with the white mist carpeting the coastline as the wild seas reached the shore. It was serene.

But far from tranquil were the scenes of the visit back I'd shared with my eldest son the previous weekend. We should have been celebrating. It was a special birthday we had returned for. As you would expect, the party, held at the local boat club, kicked off with smiles, toasts, speeches, music, and *plenty* of free-flowing alcohol for all the guests. Not a good party without plenty of alcohol, right? Towards the end of the evening, like the popping of a champagne bottle—wine fizzing and spilling out—so did the angry words escape with no control. Arguments flared between family members. I watched the charades still being played to hide the decades of unresolved heartache. But I could see through it all. Hurt people were still hurting. Glancing over to a table near the back of the room, I saw my father's familiar cold, glaring eyes, full of judgment and disdain, as he sat watching the partygoers. Sadly, he'd left his party shoes at home. Other family members, I noticed, struggling and propped up by the bar, drank their sorrows away. For some, it wasn't a time to celebrate.

What happened to the sense of family, united in love? I despondently gazed around the room.

Was I just being oversensitive? Had I been away too long? Was this their normal? Around 1 a.m., after farewelling the last guest, we returned to my sister's home, only to be greeted with more brokenness. Fragments of a smashed security camera lay scattered at the front door. Inside, more discoveries: items lay broken and strewn around the living room. Brokenness all around. Then, capping off the night, a visit from the police. My sister needed to file a report. Oh, how those childhood scenes flashed through my mind.

My heart felt like the broken security camera, my shards of thoughts and emotions like pieces of glass when I returned to Adelaide. Sitting alone at a table on the deck outside our living room, I was attempting to do my Bible study but was stopped in deep sorrow, tears flowing. Feelings I had when I was ten came flooding back—repeated history haunted my heart.

My tears left watermarks as they dripped off my cheeks onto the tissue paper. My Bible lay open to this verse.

> *Draw near to God, and He will draw near to you.* Hebrews 4:8

Then it happened. It rained. Unlike perfect pearl droplets on wax paper, the tissue pages of my Bible became rippled and weak. That was me at that moment, wavering and fragile. The raindrops joined my tears. Searching the sky, I saw not a cloud in sight. This was not a sun shower.

"How could this be happening?"

Then the Lord whispered gently to me: *I feel your pain. It breaks My heart too.* Were the raindrops tears from heaven? I could only answer *yes*. The most supernatural moment, raining down on me, was a gentle touch from my Heavenly Father, feeling my pain. He sees it all and weeps.

> I feel your pain. It breaks My heart too.

His true character revealed to us, being God as man through Jesus—a life filled with emotions, pain, and suffering—

comforted me that day with such love and tenderness. His peace showered into the pool of my mind.

The memory where the pages of my Bible and my hair got wet, where I searched the sky for the rain clouds and found none, will be forever with me. He didn't leave me wet and wondering. Moments later, with the sun still shining, I was once again dry. It was not a figment of my imagination. It happened. My pages were dry and so too my tears.

In my time of great need, marooned on my deserted island, experiencing this miraculous touch of God, I was rescued. He released me from carrying the pain of my past, knowing there was nothing I could do to change it, and He freed me from it's burden.

Reflection:

Where have your rivers of tears landed you?

How long will you wait—trapped, angry, or anxious—knowing there is One who sees and is supernaturally willing to help you?

How do destinations where you will receive peace, joy, kindness, rest, and reconciliation sound to you?

Maybe it is time to seek the Lord's help today.

16

Pastures Green

Sometimes you must hike far, climb a mountain, or take a long drive to find a green pasture. When was the last time you shed your shoes and felt the soft grass soothe your tired feet? Lay down in total relaxation, closed your eyes, and allowed the sweet scent and tender touch of the grass beneath to refresh you?

For me, the lush green pasture promised a resting place, an opportunity to be still and search for a better way. As I'd learned in Africa from the Swahili people, I needed to continue slowly and carefully, especially during another season of difficulty. There were mountains to climb, rubble along my path to negotiate, and it took a long time to find my pasture—seven years.

You recall in an earlier chapter ("Into the Storm, Seat Belts On"), I mentioned that my dad died. Then some months later, on my birthday, my sister and I received an email from the lawyers representing our siblings, advising us they were challenging our father's will.

A wise older judge arbitrated, settling the matter with a minor change to the money split. It was over.

For the next six years, I fumed inside, avoiding my half-sisters and -brothers. Deeply troubled, I rationalized my decision, telling myself logical lies. The fact that my father chose to remarry and have more children was precisely that—his choice. Did I need to have anything to do with them? No. Of course not. And especially not now that Dad was dead.

Little did I comprehend the wilderness I'd entered.

While I attempted to rid those kids from my reality, my heart would not let up. Like tumbleweeds, dry dust, and dead grasses flying around a desert, so were the thoughts about those kids floating in my mind. I felt scorched and burnt—experiencing pain—for I knew the landscape of my thinking was wrong.

> I felt scorched and burnt—experiencing pain—for I knew the landscape of my thinking was wrong.

In September, I started planning a return trip to New Zealand to visit my best friend in Tauranga. She reminded me, laughing, that I had vowed never to visit her there! I had forgotten those words, spoken in anger. Her family now lived in Dad's hometown, and after his death, so deep was my pain, I said I wouldn't ever go back.

While planning, I was doing a study of Joshua, the sixth book in the Old Testament. Moses sent the young Joshua to scout Canaan, spy on the territory God had promised would be *their* land. This was before the Jews entered it. He reported it was indeed the land of milk and honey. That is funny; New Zealand is called God's Own, the land of milk and honey.

I realized I was in this study, at that precise time, for a reason. God was doing a workout with my heart. The parallel themes were obvious to me—love, family, unity, and inheritance—as well as the theme of grace given to unworthy recipients. Reading the book of Joshua woke me to my wilderness thinking. I *was* part of a family, while I wanted to believe otherwise. That was unworthy, yet it hadn't stopped me from receiving love from my earthly father *and* my Heavenly

Father. Dad's most significant bequest to his children had not been earthly possessions, but his teaching about our eternal inheritance. The love and *grace* of God.

My family issues were over an inheritance, and it was time to get out of my desert thinking. It was desolate, dry, and barren. An atmosphere of trapped thoughts. Not a place I wanted to stay in. Now it was time to act, not react. Feeling nervous and ashamed of my behavior, I asked God for help. He showed me this. *You will go out in joy and be led forth in peace.* Isaiah 55:12 What comfort and security I received reading those words.

The outcome was beautiful. With godly courage, I visited Isaac (sister Hannah lived in Canada). Welcomed with open arms, I met for the first time his beautiful wife and three adorable little children. We enjoyed a lovely evening together. Chatting, we connected on a whole new level. It was amazing. To think I could have missed out on this beautiful family. *And* there was no mention of the past. Thank goodness.

> Having my heart no longer react out of defensive hurt was also such a relief. I could now act with love.

Driving home that night, I cried tears of relief, joy, gratitude, and love. Considering those beautiful young children, their love and acceptance of me—yes, their aunty—melted my heart even further. I was so thankful. Having my heart no longer react out of defensive hurt was also such a relief. I could now act with love. Thanks to them, my heart grew in ways I had not expected.

To this day, I am incredibly grateful God did a workout in my heart. A good shepherd guides their sheep from areas lacking food to grazing land of abundant green pastures. So was my journey. Without God's gentle guidance, rod in hand, prodding me on, I would still be roaming around in my desert of anger and resentment. Thank goodness for the stories of old. Old they may be, but life-giving they remain.

Reflection:

What are the hurts, lies, and pain you carry?

What are their effects on your life—-be honest, now?

What small steps could you take to reconcile a past hurt?

17

Secondment Abroad

This was another "out of the blue" situation I found myself in. Was this now my way of life? Absolutely. Many times, as you've already read, I found myself at another crossroad with yet another decision pending.

This short story fills in the gaps as to how we ended up living in Chicago. It was February 2017.

As I was driving home, my phone lit up. Brendan was calling. I pulled off the road. I'm sure glad I did.

"Hey, I just got off the phone with Greg. He's asked if we'd consider moving to Chicago. What do you think?"

"Wait. What?"

Hit by *that* unexpected question, I could have ended upside down in the ditch. My windscreen wipers struggled to keep the rain off the window even in superfast mode. My workout was a short and shiny forty-five minutes---but during that time, the weather had intensified. Mini rivers were raging down the gutters on both sides of the road.

Like a massive tornado picking up everything in its path, another storm—one in my mind—went wild. Questions were flying around like debris in a gale: *Move again? What about our five kids' schooling, our friends, our parents, the dog, our house? Chicago? Really?*

In my twelve years as a travel agent, I had *never* suggested Chicago as place of interest to a tourist. Going purely off news flashes and hearsay, I kept it off my dream-destination list. What was the boss thinking?

Blindsided, I had to get my focus back on the road. These Queensland tropical cyclones, you don't mess with…flash flooding and extreme winds. With water lashing up its pillars, the bridge in front was under real threat of being washed away. In the heat of the moment, it was seductive to take the fast option anyway, proceeding onto the weakening foundation. But not today. Pulling a U-turn, I began to navigate a different way home, away from the river.

What a dilemma. Choices, choices. Left, right, or straight? I had no idea what I'd find around the next corner: a fallen tree? Housing debris? More flooding?

"Oh, Lord! Get me home."

After some time, I made it off the hazardous roads. Torrents of water gushing down the drive welcomed me home. The outside steps, off a walkway to our front door, had turned into a waterfall. How I dreaded the cleanup.

As I busted inside, all eyes were on me. I stripped off my soaking jacket, a little puddle forming around my soggy shoes.

"Hey, kids. It's wild out there. We're not going anywhere today, OK!" A statement, not a question. "Now, I've got some things to do for Dad. I'll be in the office." Shutting the door behind me, I collapsed in the chair. Wow, what a morning. I felt sick. Brendan's question about Chicago opened the door to one of the most test-filled decisions of my life; there was so much at stake. Moving from New Zealand to Australia—just across the ditch—had been exciting. Moving from Adelaide to Brisbane had presented challenges, but nothing like this step: moving over nine thousand miles to America. The *yes* would affect so many, as would the *no*. A flash thought; the game show, "Who Wants to Be a Millionaire?" I needed to Phone-a-Friend.

Do I call my mum? Ha, ha. I already knew her answer. A friend?

I quickly played that tape:

Think of your kids having to make new friends and their schooling–it's different up there, and the year starts in July! DON'T DO IT. It's way too hard. The disruption is too great.

What was I thinking? Hadn't the majority of people on the planet spent their entire lives, never having moved from the town or village or state where they were born?

> Not wanting to get swept away by fear, I called my best friend, my Insurer. G.O.D– Give Order in the Decision.

Not wanting to get swept away by fear, I called my best friend, my Insurer.

G.O.D–Give Order in the Decision. I needed His divine help. To get that, I went straight to my Bible.

Yes, the homeless man I'd been chatting to that week had it right. He told me we should always check with the Big Man Upstairs. As we flippantly say, "God only knows." Of course, He does. "OK, God! I have no idea what to do."

"So, here's the deal. (Like I'm in control and can call the shots.) I'm staying put with my family unless You give me **three** obvious directives to go." Yes, I made a pact with God. If He said go, we would go. If He said stay, then stay, we would.

What a relief. Feeling let off the hook, I relaxed, knowing He would call the shots. An enormous weight off my shoulders, I experienced momentary peace. Now it was time to wait.

What happened next was wilder than the storm raging outside. It blew my mind. I opened my BSF (Bible Study Fellowship) questions. They led me to Genesis. Here was the dramatic story of Jacob, a father who for twenty-two years hadn't seen his son Joseph—his favorite of all twelve sons. The brothers' envy of his favoritism for Joseph and the coat of many colors he'd given him drove them to sell Joseph to a slave trader. They then led their father to believe he'd been killed by a wild animal, presenting false evidence of Joseph's ripped coat stained with goat's blood.

Time passed. Experiencing many years of famine in Canaan, where the family lived, Jacob learned there was grain in Egypt. He sent ten brothers to travel the great distance to buy food from the ruling governor, the pharaoh's guide and advisor; plus, he oversaw all of Egypt.

With many twists and turns, two trips back and forward to Egypt, pivoting with an unexpected revelation, the story continued. To the brothers' amazement, the man before them, they learned, was none other than their sold brother. Would their powerful brother treat them severely, with the harsh punishment they deserved? Their hatred and jealousy toward him now turned into great fear. As Joseph faithfully trusted God in his many trials, God orchestrated events to bring great blessing. Joseph's heart was full of love and compassion for his brothers. He assured them it was God's doing, sending him ahead to lead and rule in Egypt, saving the people and his family from starvation. He commanded them to go home and bring his father—the entire family, along with their flocks and herds—back for him to provide for all their needs, for the famine was going to continue for another five years. So, they did.

Upon hearing the news, Jacob was in crisis mode, having to decide. Would he pull up stakes, late in life, take the long journey into Egypt with his entire family plus livestock—at least ten days by donkey, to reunite with his beloved son, Joseph? Leave God's Promised Land, where they had so far survived famine, and journey to where Joseph was, relying on the provision of the Egyptian pharaoh? What to do?

"Heads we move, tails we stay."

Or would he take a vote, or maybe write a list of all the pros and cons? How was it possible—with all the stories in the Bible—that I arrived here with the very same question?

So, what did Jacob do, you ask? He set out with his entire family, possessions, and livestock, but before crossing into Egypt, he offered sacrifices to the God of his father Isaac, who was his faithful God. As Jacob slept, God spoke to him in a dream:

> *"I am God, the God of your father," he said.*
> *"Do not be afraid to go down to Egypt, for I*
> *will make you into a great nation there. I will*
> *go down to Egypt with you, and I will surely*
> *bring you back again."* Genesis 46:3–4

"God. Are you kidding?" I said out loud.

Shocked, I leaned back in the chair. Not only had God answered my question very clearly, but also my fear. I did not want to spend the rest of my life living away from my homeland.

Not only had God answered my question very clearly, but also my fear.

Jacob's story provided further comfort that while there would be perils in the journey unforeseen situation, God was faithful. He'd be present throughout, providing abundantly, and even turning difficulties into blessing. Facing yet another dilemma, I had to decide if I would accept this answer.

Well, let's see if there are more prompts, I told myself.

Later that week, searching for my lost earring, I pushed my bed away from the wall. I discovered something else. Lying with a gross pile of dust and a missing sock was a bookmark. I blew off the dirt particles, clothing fibers, dust mites, and hair. It read:

Carolyn's Reflections

"For I know the plans I have for you," declares the Lord, "plans to prosper you and not to harm you, plans to give you hope and a future." Jeremiah 29:11

Again, I thought to myself: *God. Are you kidding?* What a way to hear from God. The weirdest part of this story—I didn't remember ever having seen this bookmark before. I have a good memory for that sort of thing.

I didn't know whether to laugh or cry. But God again answered my fear: I would not get shot and die in Chicago. There would be no harm to myself or my family in moving to America. We would prosper, He promised—that was encouraging. It was even beginning to sound like an adventure I'd be keen to undertake. Reflecting on my story gives me goosebumps and brings tears to my eyes. I hope with all my heart you are getting this. God sees, God cares, God has a plan. And yes, God gave me clarity and order in the decision-making process. Remember "the world's mine oyster"? God is my tool for shucking unknown, tightly held questions. My family all received a highly valued pearl—wisdom on how to endure and prosper in times of trial.

God sees, God cares, God has a plan.

So, the journey continues, with tools in hand—in readiness for the next adventure.

The third prompt concerned Brendan's career. He started under the direction of his father in their small family business. He continued there under new owners after it had been sold, progressing to General Manager. The business massively expanded under his leadership. Rewarded, he received a promotion to lead another division within the company. Being easily we could allow bad news to sabotage our lives. From my perspective, Satan was having a field day. All evil comes from him. The recount of another act of domestic terror sent ripples of fear through the residents.

I love Erwin Lutzer's book *God's Devil: The Incredible Story of How Satan's Rebellion Serves God's Purposes*. He explains how we can equip ourselves against these schemes. *Knowing* Satan is critical—like that old saying "Keep your enemies close." In addition, know this: Ignorance is not bliss.

As his number-one mission, the Devil wants you to reject God—Satan wants to ambush your happiness, blinding you: a wolf dressed as a lamb; wanting you confused, stumbling through life, relying on your limited understanding. Know this: Satan's days are numbered, and he is doomed. His stealing, killing, destroying ways will one day be no more.

God, in stark contrast, is for us, with us—His number-one goal being that we have life and have it abundantly through Him forever. God has overcome Satan through Jesus— the Prince of Peace—coming as God with skin on, dying, *and* conquering death as He rose on the third day.

> God, in stark contrast, is for us, with us

But for now, being powerless against Satan and his evil ways, I will armor up. Here is an extended warning written by Paul in the New Testament:

> *This is no weekend war that we'll walk away from and forget about in a couple of hours. This is for keeps, a life-or-death fight to the finish against the Devil and all his evil angels.*
>
> *Be prepared. You're up against far more than you can handle on your own. Take all the help you can get, every weapon God has issued, so that when it's all over but the*

that he was managing a new product and it involved a new area of expertise, Brendan was in for a steep learning curve. As he faced daunting challenges, this grew his skills and character. In three years' time, that business also grew. The verse I received for Brendan was this:

> *His master replied, "Well done, good and faithful servant. You have been faithful with a few things; I will put you in charge of many things. Come and share your master's happiness!"* Matthew 25:23

Brendan, given the opportunity to run a small family business, had used his skills and talents well. His leadership had been a blessing to many within the business and the industry. He was now being offered a far greater responsibility, managing another division, this time in Chicago.

This really touched my heart. God showed me He was not only looking over my concerns, but knew Brendan was also in need of encouragement, given that this was the most formidable role in his career. This decision had reverberating effects on many lives. It was a big decision.

Reflection:

How do you reach a decision?

How would you feel, letting God help you with your choices?

Part Five

MODES OF TRAVEL

WOW! What choices for getting around we have today, and how they've changed!

I love the more recent improvements on the powered push-bike, as my dad called it. He had a little petrol tank on his bike that he could switch on to help him power up the steep hill where we lived. That was fifty years ago. Dad was ahead of his time.

Fast forward to today, e-bikes are awesome. After having the experience of riding one while visiting a cousin in Switzerland, I am very keen to invest. Anything to help this aging, repeatedly operated on body to get around. Speaking of operations, I've had my share.

18

Rocky Mountaineer Train Journey

Being a travel agent had its perks. I had the privilege of being a connoisseur of far-off places—taken around the world by airlines and tour operators, visiting amazing sites and staying at incredible hotels.

When traveling for personal pleasure, I could apply for an agent's discount for whatever mode of travel I was using—air, rail, car, cruise, coach, etc. It was a valued benefit of the job.

As a job requirement, we all had to on occasion attend industry breakfasts, where agents received updates from whoever was hosting: an airline, a coach service, a cruise line, a tour operator, etc. This usually included a giveaway as a token of appreciation. Despite the freebie, if my desk was piled high with files needing attention, such a breakfast was not welcomed.

"Good morning, everyone." An overly smiling face with a booming voice caught my attention as I gathered with colleagues at the Aura Hotel for a breakfast put on by Continental Airlines. *He's obviously had his coffee*, I thought ruefully, not having had mine.

"Thank you for taking the time, so very early"—no kidding— "to join us. You will have received a boarding pass on your way in. Please don't lose it. The number on your pass may make you that lucky person. We are giving away a free ticket to fly our friendly skies to Vancouver."

Gee, I hated these giveaways. Never won a thing in ten years. You guessed it. I wasn't much of a morning person, especially knowing the pile of work I'd left sitting on my desk.

I heard the number announced. As I glanced down at my boarding pass— expecting the usual —I felt my brain nearly explode. The winning pass! I had it. I was the WINNER. How that changed my sulky, "what am I doing here?" morning mood. I'd just won a plane ticket to Vancouver. You better believe I was going to use it.

Six months later, having planned a personal holiday to use my free airline ticket, I touched down in Canada. Having sold several trips on VIA Rail Canada Vacations, I wanted to experience for myself the wonder and magnificence of this rail journey that had been carved through the Rocky Mountains.

Excited about my next adventure, on the Rocky Mountaineer, as it is now called, I waited on the platform. Out of the rusty old speakers positioned high in the station's eves, the announcement came: "All Aboard. We depart in twenty minutes."

After the train had gently pulled out from the station, I didn't have to wait long before the dramatic scenery began to appear. The brochures hadn't exaggerated. Climbing slowly, the train weaved through lush countryside. I could see deep valleys with river canyons winding around the foothills. As it passed through long, dark tunnels and then popping out the other side, I marveled at the mountain goats that effortlessly sprang from one rock to another in search of the tufts of alpine vegetation where scarcely any was growing. Past stunning lakes of turquoise blue, we then climbed higher, through the clouds, past Mt. Robson, which at 12,972 feet (or 3,954 meters) tall sat in great majesty. What a site. Every next corner had me spellbound. Such breathtaking views of nature. What contrast existed: colors of pristine blue, green, and white; the landscape of craggy peaks and alpine meadows, frozen glaciers, and flowing waterfalls; grizzly bears and black bears; elks, caribou, moose, goats, and bighorn sheep. I was in awe.

New Zealand, my homeland, is exquisite. But this was the next level. There was grandeur all around. How could anything be so beautiful? Such pristine, unspoiled nature.

I slid the glass panel open. The hard-to-describe delights entering my nostrils gave a sense of presence, even though I was sitting on a train. Looking up, thanks to the Perspex® roof, I saw eagles hardly even flapping their wings, being lifted high on the rising air currents. I felt the enormity of the mountains towering over me. Then the sounds: the rushing water cascading over cliffs to form picturesque waterfalls; rocks falling from the cliff as a mountain goat leapt off another ledge. Journeying through this wonderland, I felt one with nature.

Then came the rain. Disappointed by the droplets on my face, I needed to close my window. After twenty minutes, bursting out from behind the puffy white clouds, the sun's warmth touched my skin. I closed my eyes and smiled. Such was the uncertainty of mountain weather. You're wet and dreary one minute. Then, around another range, out pops the sunshine.

How the rain, gifting the meadows and alpine vegetation with a drink from heaven, freshened everything up. As if having received a facelift, the greenery turned from looking bent over and limp to standing tall, seemingly looking up.

Reflecting on this incredible journey, I told myself I needed to schedule into my day every day—figuratively speaking, of course—a ride on the Rocky Mountaineer train: go see what the Creator had for me; look out and look up.

It might be as easy as walking out the back door: smelling the roses or the newly cut grass. How about taking a closer look at that massive tree in the yard, home to the nesting birds? How about observing the changing color of the leaves? Maybe it's to get up early, see the wonders of the new day. What would it look like for you?

When we refocus, we can replace the visions and feelings of fear, anxiety, resentment, anger, and all things that steal our joy and make life hell on earth. I've been at that station. You don't want to hang around there long. It's overwhelming. Not only does it suck, but it also sucks the life out of you. The passengers there—those who hurt us with their cutting words, destructive actions, and terrorizing behavior—are not who we need to travel life with. It's time to move, step on this train, and leave them behind.

> When we refocus, we can replace the visions and feelings of fear, anxiety, resentment, anger, and all things that steal our joy

Yes, you will still face the mountains and travel the valleys, but do you want a tip? When you LOOK UP, past the towering issues of life, you will see the sky. Remembering the eagle so effortlessly soaring outside my train window had me wanting to grow wings. Ever asked yourself how the eagle does this? God created these majestic birds, when all other birds flee from the storm and hide, to fly into it. They use the wind of the storm to rise higher. It takes only a matter of seconds. Added to that, they use the power of the storm and none of their own energy. Doesn't that just blow your mind? It does mine.

Look at this verse:

> But those who hope in the Lord will renew their strength.

(I can vouch for that.)

They will soar on wings like eagles; they will run and not grow weary; they will walk and not be faint. Isaiah 40:31

Can you picture yourself like this?
If no, then here's your answer.
God is waiting with open arms. He wants to embrace you, wipe away your tears, carry all your burdens, and give you wings to fly.

My Creator God talked creation into existence. He commands the heavens to open for it to rain, thunder, and send lightning bolts. God holds the world in the universe safely without having it fall off its axle. He alone sustains all He has created, and that can include you if you ask.

> He wants to embrace you, wipe away your tears, carry all your burdens, and give you wings to fly.

Now to Him who is able to do immeasurably more than all we ask or imagine, according to His power that is at work within us. Ephesians 3:20

There is a caveat; it requires us to surrender our *limited* knowledge, and admit to our faults and flaws, our humanness, and our need for God's *limitless power and love.*

Look around you. Look back in history. What remains? Rulers, nations—empires, even—have all come and gone. It is my belief, having tested it many times over, God's word remains. He is constant in a world of change, for history is His Story. He is the author. What He says happens, believe it or not.

Reflection:

What is keeping you from believing God can do immeasurable things in your life?

What is causing you to reject God?

19

Scar Ship Victorious

Have you ever experienced a cruise? A luxurious ship, exquisite meals, refined service, and exhilarating excursions onshore. It truly is all-inclusive travel. And there are many cruises to choose from: Viking Ocean Cruises, Virgin Voyages, Carnival Cruise Line, Royal Caribbean International, just to name a few.

Sadly, for me, my all-inclusive experiences didn't involve anything as wonderful. Rather, my voyages had me cruising the corridors of many doctors' hallways, had me stopping at the entrances of many medical theater "ports," and rehab excursions, where I benefited from the amazing healing hands of my physical therapists. They were the pilots of the voyage. They got me moving again, guiding me through the rough waters of rehabilitation. Hours and hours of repetitive exercise. Pole, pole steps, learning to walk again.

After four hip operations in four years, persevering through them all, I came out with new strength, new health, and joy that had been missing for the last decade brought on by constant pain. By far, the worst operation was the fourth. Talk about unwanted destinations. I hadn't seen it coming—a hip revision, this being a procedure that replaces an already replaced hip. Scared and anxious, I valiantly sailed into the unknown.

For my first hip implant, the surgeon used the metal-on-metal, MoM, prosthesis. I learned all too late that these can cause physical damage. Friction between the head and cup causes microscopic pieces of cobalt and chrome to flake off and enter the hip cavity, resulting in bone erosion, and the bloodstream, producing heavy-metal poisoning, or metallosis. These tiny metal particles can destroy bone, nerves, and the muscle surrounding the joint. This was exactly my experience.

Then I met Dave. Not letting my pain prevent me from traveling, here I was, in the Vila Nova da Gaia region, sitting high above the Douro River at Churchill's winetasting Lodge, enjoying a glass or three of their delicious port. Spotting each other's canes, we got to talking. His story was identical to mine. We were both in line for a hip revision. Dave from Ireland and I from New Zealand, worlds apart, both in Portugal— here we sat, united.

Our hip-replacement surgery had been faulty, as had happened to tens of thousands of others. We'd heard of the class-action lawsuits against the manufacturer.

Dave had registered as a claimant.

I'd considered that option. God whispered not to take on that battle. He would get me through. I believe He protected me from further anxiety, waiting months if not possibly years for an outcome. Could that rabbit hole, if gone down, destine me to more significant unexpected pain? I believed yes.

For me, the decision was simple. I trusted God—**G**oodness **O**ut of **D**isappointment, **G**reatness **O**ut of the **D**ifficulty.

On returning home, I booked the procedure. Three days after the procedure, the unthinkable happened. My hip dislocated while I stood in my kitchen. It was horrendous.

Thankfully, my daughter was home. Olivia held me upright for forty-five minutes while an ambulance, sirens blazing and lights flashing, speedily made its way to my house.

The long days and weeks that followed felt like an eternity. When sitting on my surgical chair in my shower, tears streaming down my face as the hot water washed down my back, I heard encouraging words whispered to soothe my soul: "You are My child. I love you. I see you, and I am with you. Trust Me. Lean on Me. We can do this together."

We did. Jesus's words in Romans 8:28 are true. Getting an injection of His word daily, I slowly gained strength, relearning to walk.

Through it all, I became more resilient, understood better others' pain, and learned humility as I accepted help. But patience was my most challenging side trip. Frustrated many times by the slow recovery, I still find myself bobbing up and down, paddling the patience boat.

Now standing strong, this side of good health, I am so grateful for the brilliant surgeon and his team, the equipment they used to dig the last hip out of me—quite a workshop— the new prothesis, the anesthesiologist who kept me alive, the donated bone needed to repair the hole in my joint, the donated blood for my transfusion, and I could go on.

Above it all, I am so thankful for the peace. Fear was totally replaced. Jesus, Himself a carpenter, promised that if I surrendered all my worries to Him, He would give me the peace that would surpass all human understanding. He did. I see the physical scars on my body, like fault lines on the escarpment. After six procedures, there are only three scars. Then I realized Jesus has three scars: one on each hand and one on His side. God could have raised Him without the scars of His horrifying death on the Cross. But no. It was necessary. His scars are evidence of His victory over death. Jesus died

if I surrendered all my worries to Him, He would give me the peace that would surpass all human understanding.

for me and rose so I might travel this life with Him, my very present faithful friend, and finish this life victorious, knowing I have life after death.

Viewing my scars is the evidence I have overcome. They are my daily encouragement to press on, keep moving, and enjoy this gift of life. It is a great feeling.

Cruising is wonderful. I've stepped off the Scar Ship Victorious, full of gratitude, free from pain, better and stronger. I'm banking on my next cruise to be equally memorable.

Reflection:

What are the scars in your life?

How have your scars affected your life?

How could you use your experience to encourage others?

20

Soaring High with ATT Airways

I love the relaxation of a train ride; the ease of walking around the wagon wine bar, chatting with other passengers and hearing their adventure stories. However, flying is the only way to go when traveling any distance, especially if in a hurry.

So, here's something more to know about me. My youngest child *is* a pilot. He has completed his four-year degree and is now certified to instruct students to be pilots. To pass his final test required him to intentionally stall his plane, nose-drive to the earth while spinning, and free fall. He then needed to take back control by redirecting the plane to a normal flying position and restart the engine. That is confidence right there.

I asked him what it took to be an excellent pilot.

Experience—hours and hours in the seat, tackling all obstacles, great and small

Knowledge—of the aircraft, take-off, landing, the flight plan, the weather, what to do when the unexpected happens

Ability—how to redirect when needed, get above a storm, use clear communication skills with his flight team and air traffic control, and land the plane safely, even if it means on the Hudson River.

Wow, what trust we put in our pilots, people we don't even know, most likely never see.

That's why I love taking to the skies with ATT (Almighty, Trustworthy, and True)—I can sit back and enjoy my flight, as I *know* my pilot well. He can fly me through any disaster. By believing and trusting in Him, I've seen Him in action. Yes, I am talking about God.

Remember back in Chapter 3, I talked about the importance of a name?

Did you know God has many names, all with different meanings? As I explored them, I realized I was not just learning about His names but truly getting to *know* Him: His character and His heart for me. I'll cover a few of the names so you can see why I am so willing for Him to pilot my life.

Elohim—God

In the beginning, God created the heavens and the earth. Genesis 1:1

Have you ever stopped to look at and ponder the beauty, creativity, and intricate complexity of the world we live in? I recall visiting the National Air and Space Museum of the Smithsonian Institution in Washington with William. Excitement filled our steps. Back then, William, enrolled at Purdue University in aviation training, dreamed of being a commercial pilot. We strode through the front doors with great anticipation. In wonder, our awe-filled eyes gazed upon the *Apollo 11* command module *Columbia* (the part of Apollo 11 that came back down to Earth). Also, the images of the 1984 Space Shuttle orbiter *Discovery* and the myriads of photos of the stars, the planets, and the moons floating around our galaxy. Such space phenomena. It was brought home to me even more powerfully that the space travel by NASA and other agencies to see, experience, and explore the mysteries of the cosmic world has been simply incredible. The exact number of galaxies out there has been a mystery, with estimates rising from the thousands to the millions to the billions, all as telescope technology improved.

I did a quick search; in 2016, astrophysicist Christopher J. Conselice (of the University of Nottingham in England) et al., published in the *Astrophysical Journal* an estimate that *two trillion* galaxies exist in the *observable* universe.[2]

Humanity is discovering more as technology advances, and we are far from uncovering all there is. I don't believe we will ever know, understand, or comprehend the vastness of all that our Creator God is and what He has made. We cannot enter the deepest parts of the ocean or the outer reaches of space. The power and might behind electric-storms, tornadoes, hurricanes, cyclones, tsunamis, volcanoes, and earthquakes, are all signs for us to see the Creator God. We can no more stop them than we can make them.

As we are told (Isaiah 55: 8–10), God's thoughts are not our thoughts; neither are His ways our ways. As the heaven is higher than the earth, this resembles the vast distance of thought and actions between God's perfection and human behaviors. Who is mankind to possibly think they know? No one has the capacity to know all things.

> No one has the capacity to know all things. Simply put, we are not God.

Simply put, we are not God. That said, I will take *His* advice any day and every day.

> *Trust in the Lord with all your heart and lean not on your own understanding; in all your ways submit to Him, and He will make your paths straight.* Proverbs 3:5–6

With all that said, I am fully trusting God to be my pilot. There is nothing He doesn't know, and He holds all power. Nothing is too hard for Him.

Immanuel—God is with us

I love this about God. He is *always* nearby. The Psalmist says:

God is familiar with all we do.
He knows our sitting, standing, and lying down
He knows our activities
He knows our thoughts
He knows our needs
He was there in our very making, our conception

David says this:

> *For You created my inmost being, You knit me together in my mother's womb.* Psalms 139:13

I have never experienced greater comfort than knowing God is with me.

I have never experienced greater comfort than knowing God is with me.

So do not fear, for I am with you; do not be dismayed, for I am your God. I will strengthen you and help you; I will uphold you with My righteous right hand. Isaiah 41:10

Yahweh—I AM

It is hard to comprehend—especially, as I've just detailed, with our limited capacity—the fact that God always existed, needs nothing to exist, and will exist for all eternity. This truth of God is troubling for some. Yet I take great comfort in it. My reason? He will never change, leave, or abandon me.

This name for God, Yahweh, found in the Old Testament and revealed first to Moses, was only used when He interacted with His people. He longs for us to understand He is a personal God and seeks to have a relationship with us. That really blows my mind, that He bothers with me and wants nothing more than this—a relationship—and to provide for me. That's my faith, which is not a religion; MerriamWebster's definition of "religion" is "an institutionalized system of religious attitudes, beliefs, and practices." You can't hold a conversation with an attitude, belief, or practice.

No. Religion is not for me.

Check these verses Jesus spoke in the Gospel of John:

Then Jesus declared, "I am the bread of life. Whoever comes to Me will never go hungry, and whoever believes in Me will never be thirsty." John 6:35

When Jesus spoke again to the people, He said, "I am the light of the world. Whoever follows Me will never walk in darkness, but will have the light of life." John 8:12

Jesus answered, "I am the way and the truth and the life. No one comes to the Father except through me." John 14:6

There are many verses in the Bible that tell us who Jesus is.

Question: Who do you say I AM is?

EL ROI—The God of Sight (or "the God who sees me")

This next name of God is the most comforting, I find. This week someone asked me to do a quick, two- or three-minute overview of my life. It was an amazing experience. What it showed me was that, in good times and especially in the bad, God was watching over me.

How deeply personal. He is close and watching over us 24/7 with His goodness, as He *IS* good. He sees when we are lonely, troubled, anxious, and stressed. He delights when we are full of happiness and overjoyed. He longs to help and doesn't want us to fend for ourselves, fighting our trials on our own. He wants us to draw near to Him, for He sees us and cares so much.

For the eyes of the Lord range throughout the earth to strengthen those whose hearts are fully committed to Him. You have done a foolish thing, and from now on you will be at war. 2 Chronicles 16:9

As I mentioned in Chapter 2, He saw my plight as a child. There were foolish actions resulting in a household at war. These words are so true.

He had a plan, and it was and *still* is good.

My God sees everything clearly and takes me above the turbulence, out of the clouds of trial where I get shaken, tossed around, have panic attacks,

> My God sees everything clearly and takes me above the turbulence

fearing the worst, into the clear skies above. He promises to direct my flight path. (Jeremiah 29:11)

The basic fact is we just don't know and can't see all things. We can predict but nothing is ever certain; what will happen in the next thirty minutes, let alone the next twenty-four hours, a week, a month, or a year? And what we cling to as our security can be here available one moment, then before our eyes it is gone, ruined, consumed, displaced or dissolved. Nothing on this planet lasts.

People around us are rethinking their views, looking for answers this world can't provide, as it doesn't know. Will you be one of those people? What will you do?

Reflection:

Where do you look for answers?

Whom do you put your trust in?

How steadfast is that person, bank account, investment—whatever "it" is you trust?

How ready would you be to try God in your trial? (Get Out of Disaster)

21

Bethlehem Star—Clip-clop

There he stood. Captivated, I couldn't take my eyes off him. His finely chiseled face was strong. Alert, his questioning eyes held mine, reading me and giving me 100 percent of his attention. Locked in, I moved closer. His legs, long and muscular, held him standing well above me. His nostrils flared as he continued to assess me. I reached my hand out, slowly so as not to alarm, toward his gleaming sculptured body. Gently arching his neck down, he greeted me.

Interrupted from our intimate meeting, I heard his owner's voice, "Magnificent, isn't he? Masoud is his name."

Standing under the shade-cloth for protection from the searing, dry desert sun, Amet shared their story; how he'd received the good fortune to buy him. "'Masoud' means lucky," he said.

I heard the emotion in his voice. Honored to own such a magnificent stallion, Amet could no doubt see the fondness Masoud and I passed between us in this short time as he nuzzled my back with his elegant head.

It certainly had been my lucky day. With my love of horses, I'd taken a taxi from my hotel in Giza, about nine miles from downtown Cairo, to the stables to hire a horse and ride across the dry, barren, intensely hot Sahara Desert. I wanted the adventurous option to view one of the Seven Wonders of the Ancient World—the Great Pyramid of Giza, built some 4,500 years ago. Not in my wildest dreams would I have pictured myself in my black Bedouin, colorfully patterned robe, jeans hidden beneath, astride a majestic Arab stallion attired in his finery—Arabian bridle and tasseled neck strap.

Entrusted with Masoud, I felt so privileged.

Not that this is the climax of my story, though. This is a prelude to the adventure that was to come.

Having spent the first week in Egypt, exploring Cairo alone, I joined Kumuka Tours, an adventure company specializing in unique travel options for the "wild at heart." Ten fellow adventure seekers and I relinquished the comfort of our hotel for the last ferry departure crossing the Nile. Our goal was to be the earliest group to reach our first stop.

The night sky—stars twinkly above, with the moon reflecting on the calm, still waters—overlooked the scene as, using the local ferry from Luxor, we crossed the Nile to the tiny village of Al Boaairat. I could smell the diesel from the engines below and hear low murmurings from the deckhands in a language I couldn't understand. Looking around, I saw families and couples huddled together, sleeping—propped up against the worn, weather-beaten cabin. Two a.m. should have seen me sleeping too, but I was way too excited.

As we pulled into the pier to dock, I could see the fishermen loading their nets onto their waiting *feluccas*—a type of sailboat used up and down the Nile as far back as the sixteenth century. While I was not in Israel yet—Galilee was still to come—I had visions of the disciples starting their days in the early morning, fishing.

As soon as we were back on dry land, my group leader led us down the quiet, sleepy streets to the stables. There stood Nes. ("Nes" is Hebrew for "sign," "miracle.") It was not his muscular, tall frame that caught my eye or his stellar head; he had a low hung neck, floppy ears, and sad-looking eyes. No, he was short; he didn't even come up to my chest. It was the star across his wither that jumped out at me. I thought he was no ordinary donkey. And he wasn't. He'd been well trained to take tourists up steep ascents, along narrow rocky ridge trails, and back down.

Kumuka used a company called Tour Egypt, which offered a five-hour "Donkey Ride Over the Ridge Tour" through local villages, into the desert sand to the "main" valley, Wadi al-Harim, to the ancient burial site known as the Valley of the Queens.

I settled into the bumpy, short, quick-paced gait of Nestor. The night sky was now giving way to the sun slowly rising in the far east. The small, whitewashed villages were stirring, lights turning on, and I could hear soft voices over the clip-clop of my donkey's hooves.

We had taken the adventurous option; no air-conditioned coach packed with the masses. Setting out in plenty of time, we achieved our goal. We were the first to arrive at these ancient tombs. Sure, it was the longer, less comfortable ride, but what an experience. I felt connected somehow, seeing up close the homes of the local people who lived in the small villages we passed enroute. From my saddle, I watched smoke wafting out of their chimneys and smelt the burning logs of their stoves as the morning *karkadé*, Egyptian tea, was being brewed, made of hibiscus flower petals with sweet local honey.

My ride did not disappoint, nor did the Valley of the Queens. With their authentic historic art and vibrantly colored reliefs, or wall paintings, telling the life stories of those buried there, the tombs were even more amazing than I'd imagined. At this ancient site were the burial grounds of the pharaohs' wives and children, the first dating back to the Seventeenth Dynasty, extending up through the Nineteenth and Twentieth Dynasties, 1292 to 1075 BC; the most notable being that of

Nefertari, the favorite Queen of Ramses II. Journeying back this far in history and witnessing Ta-Set-Neferu, the "place of beauty," as they knew it in ancient times, felt surreal—potent and miraculous even.

Three hours later, leaving the coolness of the tombs, I ventured back outside into the scalding heat of the midday sun. Attempting to shield myself from the desert dust I positioned my cool *shemagh* scarf over my head and wrapped it over my nose and mouth as the desert sun beat down on me. But how parched my throat was. Taking a sip from the now-lukewarm water in the flask in my backpack, I happily felt the first trickle relieve me of thirst. Past the lineup of buses and cars, there stood my little mount, humble tethered, reliably and patiently waiting. I climbed up, and we set off on our journey, the long way back to the village.

The views of the Nile in the distance were spectacular as we traversed around the ridge. Like a snake winding through the arid desert, this waterway had supplied the ancient kingdoms for centuries and still did. Nearly all the Egyptian cultural, agricultural, and historic sites have dwelt on these riverbanks. Such a contrast between the red, yellow, and creams of the rocky soils and the lush green agricultural land irrigated by this mighty river—it was a sight to behold.

Slowly, my sure-footed little donkey carried me down a steep, rocky, narrow trail past another ancient site—the Temple of Hatshepsut, the fifth ruler of the Eighteenth Dynasty.

I felt confident Nes would make it down safely. The miracle would be me not falling off. From there we made our way out of the desert terrain, back to civilization.

Dusty, thirsty, and tired, I viewed a welcome sight as we came through the village—the stables where we had started our five-hour adventure. My bum was sore, not to mention my legs, from straddling Nes's back all day. I was keen to dismount. No doubt, he was equally ready to get me off. Finding fresh water in a bucket and a pile of straw, I thanked him for an unforgettable day. After a rub between his ears and a pat on his Bethlehem Star wither, I bid farewell.

Weary from the sun's heat that evening, I collapsed onto my little single bed and thin mattress in my hotel room, my thoughts drifting back. I reflected on the humble dwellings of the locals versus the elaborate tombs of the rich and famous pharaohs' wives, their ultimate resting place; my humble donkey compared to the majestic Arab stallion I'd ridden the day prior.

My thoughts then traveled to Israel and Jesus, a true king, riding His Bethlehem donkey for the last time into Jerusalem, Palm Sunday. How humble, reliable, and steadfast He is. Nes had been to me as Jesus is to me. Jesus is the actual miracle in my life and promises me an everlasting kingdom, with no focus on luxurious tombs filled with treasures of gold, jewelry, and other items believed to be needed for the journey into the afterlife. Jesus is my treasure, and because of Him, all I need awaits me in Heaven.

Grateful for Jesus's constant care for me, I reflected on how he carried me over the rough terrain of life, up mountainous moments, where I endured pain and heartache, then down treacherous ravines of trial and tribulation. While I don't always understand or appreciate His timing, I know He faithfully works all things for good in my life, finishing with an eternal kingdom of endless peace, joy, and love.

> Grateful for Jesus's constant care for me, I reflected on how He carried me over the rough terrain of life

What a reminder. What a miracle.

Reflections:

What or who carries you through your trials?

Are they dependable, trustworthy, and there for you always and forever?

Part Six

HEADING HOME

All journeys come to an end. There comes a time to head home. It is true that nothing lasts forever. But this doesn't leave us with nothing, zip, nowt, nada. *Au contraire* (on the contrary), it opens the door to the beginning of something new.

Exciting opportunities. We get to choose.

22

Call Home

How good is speaking to a loved one while faraway? It's like having a giant cuddle wrapped with security and tied with a bow of love.

I was expecting my annual birthday call. I needed it more than ever.

But my phone never rang. My heart sank. July 6, 2009, would soon be over. I lay alone in the darkness. After a hectic day with doctors, nurses, cleaners, patients, and visitors coming and going, stillness finally rested over my orthopedic ward as the night lights dimmed my room. Occasionally, a staff-alert button ringing out interrupted the silence. It wasn't the sound I'd been waiting for. Disappointment and deep sadness swelled in my heart as I realized I would not hear from my dad on this birthday.

Over the years, Dad had had great fun, making birthday calls around the world. He'd grown a reputation for singing "Happy Birthday," ukulele tucked under his arm, to the family, friends, their children, and his ex-in-laws. An injured Russian sailor, having spent six weeks recovering at Dad's house while stranded in New Zealand, returned to Russia and received the call. Here I lay, in Australia, not so far away. Where was my call? The phone stayed mysteriously silent.

I'd been confined to a hospital only five times—in the many hours of labor. Then there they lay—my beautiful newborn babies.

Parallels with birthing a child existed; I had zero control over timing but high expectation, pushing through the pain barrier; there was a similar medical theater; doctors and nurses swarmed in and out of the room; hours later, a new arrival—this time, my replacement hip. This hospital visit, however, had me feeling one of an intruder. Out of place, I was the youngest by at least twenty years in my ward. *Thank goodness I scored a private room*, I thought to myself.

The drugs coming down the drip line were doing their job, dulling the pain. But not the excruciating, throbbing pain I felt in my heart. Nothing could block this. Right when I needed it most, my father's love eluded me. Tears cascaded down my cheeks. My thoughts recoiled me back down memory lane to my childhood. The deep well of heartache, loss, resentment, and shattered dreams and so much more. Oh, the pain. Yes, you know it. I've shared this before.

As I lay motionless on my cold, plastic-covered mattress, tubes attached to my arms, pressure bags around my ankles, the fear of pain met my slightest move; an overwhelming sense of vulnerability ran through my entire body. I felt so cold, alone, and broken.

Then I saw a little wooden cross hanging on my bathroom wall. More tears flooded my eyes and streamed down my face, dripping onto my yellow-striped, well worn, cotton hospital nightgown. Instantly, I heard the voice of my counselor: "Your heart aches with rejection, but I, your Heavenly Father, never will; you are always on My mind. I am always with you, watching over you."

> Your heart aches with rejection, but I, your Heavenly Father, never will

"God! Thank You, thank You, thank You. You *are* here. Thank You," I cried through my grief.

God's overwhelming presence filled my heart. His Holy Spirit touched my very being, calling me.

"I am here. Get-Out-of-the-Despair."

I knew the story of the cross; God took on the image of a man, Jesus, who came down from Heaven to die for me, then rose so that I could rise. In my despair, He raised me above my circumstances and the overwhelming thoughts of rejection and loneliness.

As if having grown wings while still lying alone in my bed, I felt Him lift my spirit.

That night I fell into the arms of my Heavenly Father. He operated on my broken, disillusioned heart, massaging and releasing the tension that had built over my life. I had never experienced a father's love like His.

The voice of His Holy Spirit dismissed the recorded lying voice in my head that had been on repeat since I was a little girl. I was, and am, dearly loved, wanted, cherished, seen, and heard. I'd nearly drowned at my birthday pity party. Not with beautifully chilled champagne. No. I had swallowed the cup of Satan's lies; not wanted, not good enough, forgotten.

God had heard me crying in the darkness, and He saw my pain. He was calling me with loving, outstretched arms to Himself. Yes, that image of the cross hanging on the wall.

A flash flood of thoughts broke the walls I had erected. It ended with this: "Why me?"

As quickly as this thought ran through the pathways of my mind, so came the response.

"*I am your Creator.*" (Acts 17:24)

God wanted me to know and feel His presence that night. As He tells us in Ephesians 3:16-18, I cannot escape Him, no matter where I go. His presence is always there, no matter where I find myself. He longs to fill me to the measure of *all*

His fullness, His love, forgiveness, guidance, abundance, and more. *Wow!* I cannot even imagine.

Life here is short, as Dad once told me. However, it doesn't stop here. God tells us He has prepared a special place for us to dwell for all eternity. He is returning one day to take us home, for we are heirs to His kingdom—Heaven.

That was thirteen years ago. As I reflected just now on the day the phone never rang, I looked up (I was in my office), and across the room, hanging on my mirror, another little wooden cross caught my eye—what a lovely, gentle reminder.

While time passes by, God never does. I didn't hear from my dad that day on July 6, 2009. However, I hadn't been overlooked and forgotten. I'd received a far greater call, from my Aba Father, a call from my eternal home. I hear from Him every day saying, "Come talk with me. I know you and what you need. I can help. I am here. Come sit for a while."

> While time passes by, God never does.

A resource I use daily is a book by Sarah Young, *Jesus Calling: Enjoying Peace in His Presence* (with scripture).

Remember P.A.T?

Promises from God, something to **A**pply daily, and a **T**ruth.

I want to remind you. This daily call, my security cuddle wrapped with a bow of eternal love, has my future assured. I know my Heavenly Father, and one day, when the time is right, those daily chats between Heaven and earth will stop. I'll be no longer in need. He'll have taken me home.

Reflection:

Where do you need advice and wisdom for today and tomorrow?

What area of your life needs transforming with words of life-giving power?

How does your future look?

Where are you heading?

23

Weary Traveler

Traveling can take it out of you, missing what's familiar—the comfort of your bed, friends, family, and the local café where they know your name and how you like your coffee. For these reasons and more, my heart felt drawn to New Zealand.

With my thoughts of home, preparing the last chapter's of this book triggered memories of Dad, particularly the day we talked about Heaven and earth. We'd experienced our fair share of disappointment and family grief, coming out a little beaten up. He said, "You realize we are citizens of Heaven, not earth? We are just passing through this terribly troubled and broken world. We have hope in all that awaits."

Those words still hit hard, as I never got to say goodbye to Dad. He couldn't have scripted them better, given that he didn't know he was soon to meet his Maker. God only knew.

Thankfully, I've found freedom from the pain of his passing. His words confirm he'd gone ahead, and I know I will see him again. Time spent together here on earth was like a kaleidoscope—constantly changing, with many shafts of different colors and shapes. As the days, months, and years turned, so did the images left behind. Some are beautiful, while others range from ordinary to gloomy to monochrome, stripped of all color. Turbulent times had made us all weary.

However, Dad's words not only gave me freedom from past pain, but also taught me the answer to death—God's perfect Kingdom, no pain, heartache, division, illness, or suffering. Only love and joy exist. What a reunion that will be. This weary traveler journeys on with this peace in her heart.

> God's perfect Kingdom, no pain, heartache, division, illness, or suffering.

I have another home that awaits my true destination. Dad showed me the pathway to get there. Jesus *is* the way. He declared it Himself.

> *"I am the way, the truth, and the life. No one comes to the Father except through me."* John 14:6 (NKJV)

That is the reason Jesus came—to conquer sin, guilt, and death so that whoever believes in His saving grace will live for all eternity in peace and unity, together with God our Father. Here is how this truth is presented in The Message translation[3]:

> *But let me tell you something wonderful, a mystery I'll probably never fully understand. We're not all going to die—but we are all going to be changed. You hear a blast to end all blasts from a trumpet, and in the time that you look up and blink your eyes—it's over. On signal from that trumpet from Heaven, the dead will be up and out of their graves, beyond the reach of death, never to die again. At the same moment and in the same way, we'll all be changed. In the resurrection scheme of things, this has to happen; everything perishable taken off the shelves and replaced*

*by the imperishable, this mortal replaced by
the immortal. Then the saying will come true:
Death swallowed by triumphant Life!
Who got the last word, oh, Death?
Oh, Death, who's afraid of you now?
It was sin that made death so frightening
and law-code guilt that gave sin its leverage,
its destructive power. But now in a single
victorious stroke of Life, all three—sin, guilt,
death—are gone, the gift of our Master, Jesus
Christ. Thank God!* 1 Corinthians 15:55–
57 (MSG)

Are you exhausted, traveling through life? God doesn't want us weary, anxious about our next challenge, our next move, our tomorrow.

With no knowledge of what is next for Brendan and me, once this "secondment" abroad comes to an end, we ask these questions in our minds, but also in discussions with family and friends: Will we be transferred somewhere else? Will Brendan retire, and if so, to where?

This one thing I *do* know. God has us covered. I just need to reflect over the last twenty-five years away from New Zealand.

Remember the very personal bookmark I discovered under my bed? God knows and has a plan. I don't mind repeating what I've written earlier, and I hope you don't mind hearing it again. Here is His extended promise, one I have experienced repeatedly:

*"I know the plans I have for you," declares the
Lord, "plans to prosper you and not to harm
you, plans to give you hope and a future.*

Then you will call on Me and come and pray to Me, and I will listen to you. You will seek Me and find Me when you seek Me with all your heart. I will be found by you."
Jeremiah 29:11–14

Experiencing many trials, only some of which I've shared, made me a weary traveler. However, I've learned to trust in Jesus. He is my best friend, and along with the Holy Spirit, who lives in my heart, has taught and guided me. I journey on, still needing to combat fear and trials that present, confident in God's unchanging love for me. I focus not on the size of my trial, but on the size of my God. Nothing is too big for Him.

> I focus not on the size of my trial but on the size of my God.

There will be further trials before my time is done. I have the truth; He died and rose again, proving how much He loves me. He was victorious over death, so I live in the power of this knowledge. You can trust me when I say it is powerful.

So, when I'm *really* weary, the lyrics of Josh Groban's song fill my head and filter down to my heart. If you, like me, need encouraging, I can recommend listening on YouTube to his song "You Raise Me Up."

I *love* how the Lord sees me where I am. So grateful for His whispers, gentle calling, nudging, and prodding, I go to be encouraged and renewed in this place of quiet, sitting with Him.

He raises me up to climb that next mountain. I am not swallowed up by the sea swells; rather, I walk on top of life's storms and seas. When the next step is too great, I know He will carry me on His shoulders, so I can be more than I could be, struggling on alone.

Reflection:

What messages fill your mind, dragging you down?

Where do you go in search of answers?

What do you do when weary and exhausted?

Have you thought of searching the Promises of God for renewal?

24

Homeward Bound

What defines home? Here's a precious definition I found while chatting with a fifth grade boy: "Home means an enjoyable, happy place where you can live, laugh and learn. It's somewhere where you are loved, respected, and cared for. Home is where your heart is."

After twenty-five-plus years of living away from New Zealand, Brendan and I have had many conversations about going "home." Based on the little boy's description, that could be anywhere. But where?

Here's our problem—too many choices. Maybe the inviting sandy shores of the Sunshine Coast in Queensland, Australia, with our existing family address an hour away in Brisbane. Or maybe in South Australia, where our eldest son has just purchased his first home. But what about the other children? Is it possible to design our retired years based on where they live? That's no longer possible: one being Australia, three *currently* in the USA, and one in New Zealand.

What about sunny Hawks Bay, North Island, New Zealand, our homeland, which still boasts lots of open green, uncultivated countryside and where people snap up rental cottages? We have lots of Deck family there. Everything is only twenty minutes away; beautiful vineyards and beaches, great cafés serving wonderful coffee. There's an added bonus; the family bach on the bay of Lake Taupo, only two hours away. That *would* be fun. Then there's Christchurch, on the South Island—close to my family; mother, sister, niece, and great nieces. More beautiful beaches and mountains.

Following these last seven years of high-rise apartment living (on the forty-fourth floor), watching glorious sunrises; storms rolling in, then enclosed with clouds—some might even say with my head in the clouds—a little house on the prairie sounds inviting; a homegrown veggie patch; picking apples off the trees; happy, free-running chicks laying healthy eggs; walks with the dog. Yes, it must be suitable for our Freddie; he must come. The point of this story—my life journey so far with its stopovers, destinations, trials, and difficulties—life is full of choices. As I'd overheard my wise husband tell his staff, "With every choice there is a consequence."

Brendan and I have jointly made decisions a-plenty, with enormous consequences, as you have read.

Could there be a lens into tomorrow to find our happy home? That's a big question.

Answer: We team up with God. He invites those who feel weighed down with pressure, decisions, worries, and in fact anything lodged in their minds, to go to Him and wear His yoke and learn from Him—gentle and humble in heart—for there you will find rest. (Matthew 11:28–30)

Let me explain: a yoke, or wooden bar, is used to join animals like oxen at the head or neck so they can pull together.

> God has no burdens, so He takes all the weight.

Here's what is great about this. God has no burdens, so He takes all the weight. We just need to walk alongside, rest up, and learn His way. When we do, He refocuses our visions, removing the fog, to align with His perfect perspective, giving us the fullness of life we dream of having.

No one can know the future except Him, and He promises to equip us with all we need. His gift, we can find no place else. What incredible hope and assurance I have concerning the future. I'm excited and full of expectation, especially in view of the last twenty-five years. I can tell you, being yoked with the Lord away from my homeland has been a wild ride.

Brendan and I have lived through such contrasting seasons—winter with sadness, heartbreak, sickness; spring with hope, new beginnings, and opportunities; summer with fresh growth, the need for protection, and an abundance of activity; and fall with successes and achievements and failures. Such fullness of life. My faith doesn't prevent me from experiencing all life throws at me. Rather, God promises to be with me to walk through the difficulties and come out better. Yes, all seasons He uses for my good. As I've learned His ways. I've experienced mental, physical, and emotional rest, release from anxiety, and freedom from deep pains in my past. Living and walking with Him has given me the best roadmap I could ever wish for.

Wherever our retirement home location, I'm ready, confident it will be wonderful.

Reflections:

What have the seasons of life looked like for you?

How have you fared through it all?

Where do you go to seek guidance for your future?

How does your guide, escort, chaperone match up to mine?

25

Where is the Promised Land?

Genesis, the first book in God's "Love Letter" to us, started with the brilliance of life and ended with the reality of death. Throughout this book we hear God telling people of the future with full authority and prophecy, not guesswork. God not only told what would happen, but He made it happen, His way and in His timing. This is history: His Story. So not only was God in the past, He is here today, and already in the future.

Blocked by uncertain and inclement weather, the sun won't be visible every day. Does that mean there is no sun? Of course not. God is no different.

I know God is always there. He is for me. He loves me. He has always provided for me. He has never failed me. One day, He will return for me.

I am unique, on the one hand, and on the other, my story is no different from anyone else'. I've experienced love, joy, celebration, triumph, success, the miracle of birth, and by contrast, brokenness, disappointment, divisions, unexplained and inconceivable pain — "pits" and "prisons." But I can promise you one thing. *Nothing* went unnoticed by God.

> *Nothing* went unnoticed by God.

None of my pain was wasted. God, as He promised, used it for good. Was it hard? Yes. Did it hurt? Yes. I experienced hours, days, weeks, months and even years of pain in my joints resulting in six hip operations, including three new hips. That's just a partial list of physical endurances. Along with them came plenty more emotional, mental, and spiritual stresses, starting in my childhood and continuing into my adult life.

The Bible states that God uses all things for good for those who love Him and for His purpose. What was my outcome? I was reshaped and adjusted. My thinking and my heart underwent enormous change. I had to learn new things while giving up others.

After all my operations, my daily routine changed for a time—requiring hours of rehab and rest. With each passing day, I grew stronger. Through it all, God's comfort sustained me. Those days spent crying, feeling sorry for myself and wondering why, wanting to give up, I knew and felt His presence.

Through the season of pain, change happened—a newness of life. I can now walk the lake, not just the block. With my heart conversion, I can pick up my phone and call my brother. I can have hard conversations without losing my cool. I am grateful for it all. In a nutshell, I was transformed.

There is only one place free from all pain and suffering: the Promised Land, Heaven. I've talked already about my conversation with Dad regarding our citizenship. After his death I bought a "rock of remembrance" (Joshua 4:1–7) I wear around my neck every day. Dad gave me the understanding that as a child of God, I am a citizen of Heaven, my Promised Land.

Look around. Is not the world broken? There is so much I don't know and have no answer for. Actually, no one does. These unknowns only draw me closer to this verse:

Trust in the Lord with all of your heart, and
lean not on your own understanding; in all

WHERE IS THE PROMISED LAND?

your ways acknowledge Him and He shall direct your paths. Proverbs 3:5–6

I don't want to sound sadistic, but let's be honest. Death is a significant, inevitable part of life. While it can be difficult, upsetting, and uncomfortable, it is necessary to talk about it, ask questions, and have a plan. Being able to demystify the fear and anxiety about death is a good thing.

> for God has a plan for life **and** death.

It truly is a good thing, for God has a plan for life *and* death. He is the roadmap to the Promised Land, where there is eternal life free from all pain and suffering, and full of life and love and abundance—Himself. His Promised Land will be my ultimate destiny.

Reflections:

Have you given any thought to what happens after death?

What is your plan?

Now that you know mine, will you join me?

26

Not the End of the Journey

I used to think the unexpected turbulence that resulted in so many fears, leaving too many questions and unknowns—what if, if only—existed simply to take the wind out of my sails. As the motion sickness waged war in my life, I felt like a cork tossed around in the tide of turmoil. On the surface, that description appeared true.

What *was* true were the storms. Truth be known, though, we have choices and, most importantly, the freedom to determine what we think and how we respond. Repeating myself again, let me remind you that

let me remind you that while free to choose, we are not free from the consequences.

while free to choose, we are not free from the consequences.

Greatness Out of the Despair, Disappointment, Devastation, Dysfunction, Disapproval, Disaster, or Dilemma is possible with G.O.D. Being the Creator God He is, there is little wonder He knows how His designs are to work, function, survive, and thrive.

The instruction manual for life, Basic Instruction Before Leaving Earth, the Bible, doesn't leave us guessing. No. He makes clear how to live and love well. The consequences for breaking His design, He outlines, warning of the outcomes. Yes, there are consequences.

Abundantly clear is His answer to restoration and wholeness. Once we are shattered, broken, crushed, and separated, God restores through His Son Jesus. Our future is secure.

There is no answer that parallels God's hope for all that happens after life on this earth.

Last time I checked, there is a 100 percent mortality rate. What we know will end, but it isn't the end.

Jesus showed me He *is* the Light of the world. He illuminated His light into the dark cavern of my life where pain, sorrow, disappointment, anger, and brokenness all hang out. We walked the roadmap together.

He knew the way forward, saying when and where to go and when to stay. While I was alone and suffering, He comforted my aching heart. His words took me out of the turmoil and into His truth. I learned to trust Him. Following His gentle lead, I left the darkness behind; out of my self-pity and self-indulgence, thinking I knew the way. I saw myself in a new light. He called me His child.

While this little girl had emerged out of a broken, messed-up family, this did not define my life. He showed me that was not the end of my story. I received not only a lamp for my feet, reading the Bible each day, trusting in His ways, but also God's abundance from above: joy, peace, unity, laughter, and most of all—*love*.

We are the children of our parents. As you know, my parents' relationship ended in sorrow and heartache.

Thankful for Jesus's love for me, I've been adopted into God's Family, greatly loved and fully accepted. He tells me my future is guaranteed, a home forever with Him. In the instruction manual for life, the Bible, we read that the future is determined. History is His Story. He was in my past, I know His presence walking with me today, and am assured of hope for tomorrow and all eternity. Ripley's "Believe it or Not!" God gives us the choice, but what we may believe, remembering the hidden lie, does not make His existence any less true.

My adoption makes me a citizen of Heaven. Let me paint the picture of my new home as God's word tells us. It is amazing beyond what we have even seen or known here on earth. Want to know more? It has:

- No pain, brokenness, sorrow, sickness
- No tears
- No death
- No evil, crime, or thieves
- No hardship, toil, or suffering
- No more anger, rejection, grief, heartache, depression, loss
- No more living in a broken body or a broken world

Heaven is:

- Out of this world
- Where our Loving Father lives and reigns
- A perfect place designed for us
- Life for infinity and beyond
- His perfect home with forever love
- A physical place with streets, homes, trees, water, animals
- Where delicious food awaits our pleasure
- Where Treasures are stored up for us, never to decay or be stolen
- Where our bodies will be perfect and strong
- Where I'll still be the recognizable me
- Where we have no hang-ups, fears, mistakes, resentment, anger, burdens, jealousy, and NO worries
- Where I'll reunite with my family and friends who trust and love the Lord

Know what I love about God? I have traversed deserts, the wilderness. I've taken the wrong road, missed a few planes, landed myself on an uninhabited island. But He was always there; in the boat with me while it stormed all around. Yes, He allowed those storms.

I hear you asking, "Why? Why so much pain?" The answer: so I would trust Him, thereby experience His provision…*peace* in the turbulence, *strength* in the trial, *restoration* in the brokenness, *confidence* in the chaos. More, He wants me to know He is God: all-powerful, all-knowing, forever present. His mercies start afresh each day. He sees my mess-ups, loves me anyway, and turns my failures into victories.

> experience His provision…**peace** in the turbulence, **strength** in the trial, **restoration** in the brokenness, **confidence** in the chaos.

I'm so grateful, for I know there will be more storms to come. With Jesus as my pilot, I hear His gentle, peaceful voice: "Ladies and Gentlemen, this is your pilot speaking. As you can see out there, a formidable storm is raging. I have been through these and seen them thousands of times before. So, don't worry. For now, take your seats and fasten your seat belts. Sit back, relax, and enjoy the flight."

My pilot through life's storms, and my ever-present friend, He assures me:

> *"I've told you all this so that trusting me, you will be unshaken and assured, deeply at peace. In this godless world you will continue to experience difficulties. But take heart! I've conquered the world."* John 16:33 (MSG)

Hearing these words is a constant reminder I need not worry.

Looking in the rear-view mirror of life, I see my journey. I received a new flight path. He helped me overcome and will do it again, always there with every new adventure and unexpected storm. As I look ahead through the wide-open windshield, my future is secure. With God's help, I'm going to keep flying high, wind in my hair above the turmoil, with visions of Heaven, until the journey's end.

One day, I will take my last breath. One day, my heart will stop beating. One day, my life will end. On that day, I'll no longer need my New Zealand passport for my sixteen-hour flight home. I will get a one-way ticket. In the blink of an eye, I will be there.

My Heavenly Father, standing at the door of Heaven, will welcome me home.

In the beginning, God—created me with a beating heart and breath in my lungs. In the end, God—will take me to my forever home with a new resurrected spiritual body to start a new life and a new adventure; only, this time no more turmoil. Landed—high above, forever home.

I pray with all my heart that one day you too will have received your one-way ticket. He is waiting. Wind in our hair, we will arrive home for good in the calm and perfect faith above the turbulence.

Reflection: *one last question*

Have you considered and planned for the long term…what happens after all this??

ACKNOWLEDGMENTS

Before I go anywhere, I want to say, Thank You, Lord. I wouldn't be here without You, Creator and sustainer of all that exists. Each breath I take is a gift from You. Thank You for being the author of my story. I owe it all to you.

Brendan, I want to honor you. No day passes when I don't love you more. I look at us and wonder: How can this be? But God. What a crazy, wild ride it has been from the beginning: I, your travel agent. You, as my husband, are the greatest blessing of my life—beyond my wildest dreams. Your support, in and out of the turbulence, loving me with that enormous, generous, forgiving heart, has seen me land here in one piece. I am so excited about the destinations ahead, you by my side. Thank you for loving me as you do. We will be together for now and forever. Amen.

Jeremy, Adam, Harry, Olivia, and Will, you kids have blessed me with abundance. You've taught me how to love better; push through adversity; be strong; broaden my mind; take risks; travel light, and journey through life, looking to new horizons. It delights my heart whenever we come together from around the world to sing, dance, laugh, and even cry. I am ridiculously proud to be your mum. Thank you for your love and encouragement. You are the best! I love you all so very much.

Dad, you have left this world, but I know where you are, saving me a spot. Thank you for sharing your love of Jesus, so I can join you one day. But not too soon, as there is much to do here. Our journey was difficult, but you taught me such lessons. Yep, through hard knocks and travel. Thanks to you, I have a passion for people and this giant world of sport and adventure. Until we next meet, Dad, love you.

Mum, you are my inspiration. You've survived many dark, bumpy, and lonely rides. Persisting along the unknown path, you've held Jesus's hand and witnessed His promises through it all. Your trials are testimony to His love traveling out of each storm. You have taught me to trust Jesus, and I thank you with all my heart. I love you dearly.

Deb—the best sister a little girl could ever want—your love for me has never failed. From those scary, troublesome nights as children, your sacrifice in raising your teenage sister when first married; sharing the highs and lows of birthdays, marriage, and death; celebrating life in the hot tub, wine in hand—thanks, Pete—and so much more. Thank you with every fiber of my being. God knew I needed you as my big sister. Here's to making memorable trips together wherever they may be. Love you lots.

The Bowling Family—now multiplied in size. Betty and Lowell. Thank you for taking the risk of bringing me into your home: the unknown schoolgirl from New Zealand. Your lives taught me to love well, no matter the circumstances, have hard conversations, be gracious and forgiving, and listen with my heart. While still learning, I have carried these examples on into my life. Thank you, sisters Lori and Kim, you generous, accepting souls, for sharing your home, your lives, and your faith with me. And you too, Bob, the big teaser of my twelve months! You all impacted this Kiwi girl's life forever. I am so eternally grateful.

To my Willow Family. Amy for answering the phone the day I called. Listening to a stranger's need, then asking me to lunch. It all started with you. You're an angel.

Thank you Pastor Rob and the Team for the Transform Series, where this book was birthed; prior to this, nothing but a blank page. Tammy, you were the first person I told when called into this scary adventure. Your invitation to become writing buddies got me started, removing my fear. Thank you for the months and now years of support. To my many small-group friends. Thank you for your encouragement, wrapping me in your love and prayers, especially when I was lost in the process.

To my writing friends at Hope*Writers, Christian Book Academy, and Self Publishing School. This slow-learning student needed you *all*. To my extraordinary 2022 Writer Team Progress ladies. Thank you, girls, for sharing this journey with me.

To Margaret Harrell, my magnificent editor. From your first email, I knew you were the one. Your expertise and patience have been extraordinary. The referral was everything they said and so much more. You have breathed life into my words, having them sparkle on the page. Thank you.

Finally, to my friends around the world. Your encouraging comments and emoji likes, hearts, and thumbs-ups on Facebook and Instagram have kept me going. I am incredibly thankful for your support and for sharing my message. Love you all.

APPENDIX 1

My book is an invitation for you. Come, meet my best friend, Jesus, His Heavenly Father, and the Holy Spirit. There is a seat at the table, a place just for you *now*, and an eternal home waiting. (For those who know Him already, *please don't walk away. If you are tempted, pray this littler prayer.*)

...silently or out loud, either way, He hears you.

Dear Lord Jesus,

Oh, how I need you.
I am weary and tired of living life my way.
I am exhausted with worry and fear for my future.
I am over living for myself.
I am more than just sorry.
I recognize I have hurt myself, others, and You.
I ask You to forgive me.
I want to walk away from my burdensome choices.
I want to journey life with You, my Savior, from now on.
I ask You to take control. You be my pilot.
I ask You into my life so I may live my life for You.
Help me trust You to do things Your way.
These things I ask in Your Name, Jesus.
Amen

If you have just prayed this little prayer, know this. God and all the angels of Heaven are singing right now.

Your decision to say yes is, hands down, the most important, powerful, and wisest choice of your entire life. I am so excited for you. *Be sure to email me.*

Now buckle in. The journey has just begun. You're in for the trip of your life, living with hope until you reach your final destination, Heaven.

I just want to point out something very important before moving on. Yes, I repeat myself; I believe you might need a reminder. You have not entered a religion, driven by what you *have to* do to reach an *acclaimed* destination. Oh no. As Jesus said just before He died on the cross, "It is done." This is why I say you can live *light*, handing your troubles to Him; why I say you can live unburdened and *free*, because He takes away the wrongs of yesterday and has paid the price so you are debt free; it is why I say you can live a *fearless* life, because Jesus's love for you drives out *all* fear.

Besides, you will be walking with the Almighty, all-knowing, all-powerful God who adores you. He is mighty to save, and He does. You need not fear today, tomorrow, or where your final destiny will be. It is *assured*. God is for you, and Jesus will fight every battle with you, against the evil of this world. And one day He will return and take you home. There is *no* other that can match Him. You have started a relationship with the Almighty Jesus. He is the only God who came down from His high place so you could walk and talk with Him. He is alive and well and is waiting. He is available 24/7.

As with any new relationship, you need time to get to know them—there are four in your new relationship: you; **Jesus**, your friend; your **Heavenly Father**, your provider; and the **Holy Spirit**, your guide. You need all three.

Best friends listen and talk. They share happy moments and comfort in difficult times. They go out together, have fun, celebrate, dine, and hang out.

Jesus is no different. Know He will always be there. When you feel like He is absent, not taking your calls, know He *is*. You may have become too busy, forgetting to check in with Him.

Here are *some* keys to growing in your faith:

Come to Him daily with a humble heart, earnestly seeking His guidance in every situation.

Start and finish your day quietly with Him, talking, (aka–prayer), with thanks, praise, and requests, (pour out your heart asking for His help) but remember to listen, not just talk. That's why God gave us two ears.

Along with prayer, read the Bible, known as the living word, God talking to you. Here, He reveals His promises to guide and provide wisdom when you seek *and* surrender to His lead. I'd suggest a Study Bible that helps fill in the gaps with footnotes and sectional headings to give understanding as you reflect on the passages. I love The Jeremiah Study Bible (NIV): *what it says, what it means, what it means for you*. Dr. David Jeremiah has some of the soundest teachings I've come across. Check out www.DavidJeremiah.org

Where to start? 1 Peter, his first letter to persecuted Christians: how to grow up in faith, know your real identity as a child of God; know where your hope comes from, how to behave, how to cope with suffering; and know your unshakable destiny. There is such wisdom packed into this little book of just five chapters. An excellent resource would be *10 Keys to Unlock the Christian Life* by Colin S. Smith.

Having read some of my trials, you'll know the road will not be smooth. You will need a team, a community of support. God uses their wise counsel to direct you. Remember, we are the average of the five people we hang with. You'll need other Christians with the experience of traveling this ever-changing world. A great Jesus-focused church is essential. You will discover the support you need through the ministries of worship, sermons, serving teams, small groups, and more.

Here's a warning. Satan is angry right now. He is against God; hates, despises, and wants to destroy anyone associated with Him. You have caught his attention. Read Chapter 12 as a refresher. However, *fear not*. He is a created being, and no match for the Creator God. Our weapons against him are far greater. (Ephesians 6:10–19) Dress daily in the armor God has provided. Remember, heavenly assistance is only one prayer-word away: HELP!

This is not the end of the list, but I will stop here. We journey on with God's Spirit, the spirit of *peace*. He promises and provides unexplainable peace when we follow His direction and walk in His ways.

APPENDIX 2

In Chapter 6, "Take Your Charger and Adapter," I referenced Bible verses and material I've used as my tools to help me along the twists and turns, and turbulence of life. This is not an exhaustive list. Rather, a starting point. My hopes and prayers are that you use them to steer your life, keeping you from heading in the wrong direction, and that they lend you with the encouragement you'll need during times of trial.

The trek through life has us constantly influenced by worldviews. There are old and new ways of thinking and interacting within social and global communities, taking us further into isms of the age; nationalism, capitalism, imperialism, liberalism, abolitionism, racism, sexism, realism, impressionism, globalism, socialism, and so it goes on. These ideologies are human created. They are flawed, for none of us has full understanding of anything, and if any claim to, *run!*

This is why I take God as my authority, the Creator of all things. He knows. He promises to lead us along the right path, together, for He alone has the answers. We can trust God with what we cannot understand.

May this small list be a start for you in discerning the truth as you apply it to your life, where you can live in the fullness of His *certain* promises. His word is truth, (John 17:17) and what He says happens. He wants the BEST for you.

Bible Verses: *The New King James Version*
(Selected from my precious Bible, a wedding gift from my father-in-law)

Pray *first*, asking the author, God, to reveal to you what He wants you to hear, know, embrace, and apply. This is His love letter to you. Enjoy reading from different Bible translations. This helps understand the passage.

LOVE
Jeremiah 31:3 *The Lord has appeared*
John 3:16 *For God so loved the world*
Romans 5:5 *Now hope does not*
Zephaniah 3:17 *The Lord Your God*

TRUST
Jeremiah 29:11 *I know the plans*
Psalm 105:4 *Look to the Lord*
Proverbs 3:5 *Trust in the Lord*
Psalm 91:1-2 *He who dwells*

HOPE
Psalm 32:8 *I will instruct you*
Psalm 139:7–10 *Where can I go*
Romans 8:38-39 *For I am persuaded*
Luke 1:37 *For with God nothing is*

FEAR
Isaiah 43:1-5 *Fear not, for I*
Psalm 31:19-20 *I will be glad*
Psalm 56:3-4 *Whenever I am afraid*
John 14:1-2 *Let not your heart*

PEACE
Psalm 46:10 *Be Still*
Isaiah 54:10 *For the mountains*
John 16:33 *These things I have spoken*
Philippians 4:7 *and the peace of God*

LIFE
Romans 12:2 *Do not conform*
Proverbs 4:4–7 *Let your heart*
Matthew 6:25-27
Isaiah 43:18–19 *Do not*

TRIAL
Proverbs 3:6 *In all your ways*
Psalm 34:17–18 *The righteous*
Psalm 46:1 *God is our refuge*
Matthew 11:28–30 *Come to Me*

HELP
1 Peter 5:7 *Casting all your I*
James 4:8a *Draw near to God a*
Psalm 34:6 *The poor man*
Isaiah 41:10 *Fear not for I am*

FAITH
Proverbs 3:7 *Do not be wise*
Psalm 28: 7–8 *The Lord is my*
Exodus 33:14 *He said*
Joshua 1:5,9 *No man shall be*

JOY
John 17:13 *I have given them*
Romans 15:13 *Now may the*
Psalm 16:11 *You will show me*
Colossians 2:2-3 *That their*

Reading Material:

Jesus Calling: Enjoying Peace in His Presence by Sarah Young
Experience God's Power through Prayer by Rick Warren
Finding God in the Margins by Carolyn Custis James
Everyone Always by Bob Goff
Is This the End? by Dr. David Jeremiah
Fear Is Not the Boss of You by Jennifer Allwood
Wonderfully Made by Allie Marie Smith
What on Earth Am I Here For? by Rick Warren
The Last Hour by Amir Tsarfati
The Road Back to You by Ian Morgan Cron and Suzanne Stabile
When Your World Falls Apart by Dr David Jeremiah
Captivating by John and Stasi Eldredge
Seeing through Heaven's Eyes by Leif Hetland
My Daughter, My Daughter by Dee Brestin and Lori Beckler
How Are You, Really? by Jenna Kutcher
Deeper by Dane C. Ortlund
Draw the Circle by Mark Batterson
Life without Lack by Dallas Willard
Managing Leadership Anxiety, Yours and Theirs by Stev Cuss

APPENDIX 3

By the greatest of good fortune, it just so happened that at a writers' conference I met Eric Mills. As he shared, one night around the fire-pit, his story and vision to be an advocate with his wife Susan, for a precious group of orphaned kids and widows, it touched my heart. Then he made a comment that *hit* my heart deeply: "Join the dots." Gazing into the flames dancing before me, I *joined* the dots. In front of my eyes, I saw my own memories: those gorgeous little faces, smiling at me when I collected sticks on the Serengeti Planes, to seeing my daughter's photos, taken when she went with Habitat for Humanity to build houses for AIDS orphans in Malawi.

Once again, I felt the impact of those beautiful faces of the women and children, vulnerable, fighting to survive.

Eric told me he and his wife were inviting others to join them in serving; providing practical and holistic strategies, as well as resources to care for orphans and widows in Uganda, and beyond.

Psalm 147:4 God determines the number of the stars and calls them each by name.

And so birthed Faces with Names International.

It is my honor and privilege, using the funds from my book, to make an eternal difference in an individual life, a face with a name, giving each orphan and widow a HOPE and a FUTURE.

Here is a letter from Eric.

Dear Friends,

Thank you for the opportunity to invite you to be a part of the exciting work God has called us too, in Uganda through Faces With Names International.

Our mission is to help orphans and widows move beyond a life of survival, and thrive, to fulfill their God given purpose.

As I have had the opportunity to meet these precious kids and widows face to face, to learn their names, hear their stories, I am compelled to advocate on their behalf.

Our desire as an organization is to create a holistic approach and depth of care, which will allow each individual child and widow to thrive. This approach requires us to meet the ongoing and basic needs of proper nutrition, clean water, medical care, a proper education, all in a safe living environment and built on the foundation of Christ.

As we are able to establish consistency in these basic areas for each individual, we believe we can then build life and leadership skills, to support their physical, emotional and spiritual development, and help them fulfill their God given purpose.

Our vision is this: To allow you, the opportunity to care for orphans and widows in their distress.

You can make an eternal difference in an individual life, a face with a name, by

partnering with us, and giving each orphan and widow, a HOPE and a FUTURE!
Will you join us?

Go to faceswithnames.org to learn more and partner with us.

Cheering You On In Christ,
Eric Mills

President
Faces With Names International

NOTES

1. Stephen A. Diamond, PhD, "How Mad Was Hitler?" https://www.psychologytoday.com/us/blog/evil-deeds/201412/how-madwas-hitler.
2. "Two Trillion Galaxies, at the Very Least," *The New York Times,* Two Trillion Galaxies, at the Very Least - The New York Times (nytimes.com); Ethan Siegel, "This Is How We Know There Are Two Trillion Galaxies in the Universe," This Is How We Know There Are Two Trillion Galaxies In The Universe (forbes.com) ; Christopher J. Conselice et al., "The Evolution of Galaxy Number Density...," THE EVOLUTION OF GALAXY NUMBER DENSITY AT z < 8 AND ITS IMPLICATIONS - IOPscience.
3. 1 Corinthians 15:51–58, The Message, 1 Corinthians 15:51-58 MSG - But let me tell you something - Bible Gateway.

THANK YOU FOR READING
My Book
Above the Turbulence

I hope the experiences I've shared encouraged
you to discover purpose in your past and the
courage to live a fearless and free future.

I'd really love to hear your feedback.

Please take two minutes now to leave a helpful review
on Amazon, letting me know your thoughts.

Thanks so much!!

Carolyn Deck

ABOUT THE AUTHOR

Carolyn Deck, a Kiwi, (New Zealander), is passionate about life. She loves all things family, travel, adventure, and sport. Her love for Jesus, she shares with everyone; the doorman, the fellow dog owner, the taxi-driver, family and friends. She has been blessed with traveling the globe over her lifetime. As a teenager, she left the debris of her derailed family home in New Zealand, traveled abroad as an international student, and spent twelve months in the United States. Upon her return, she embarked on a career in the travel industry, becoming an Area Manager in her mid-twenties. Carolyn has spent twenty-five years away from her homeland, visiting over twenty countries while living in Australia and America, and will continue to do so with her best friend, husband Brendan. Presently living in Chicago, along with adult children Harry and Olivia, she has William in Charlotte, North Carolina, Adam in the Hawks Bay, New Zealand, and Jeremy in Adelaide, South Australia. Travel is not going to stop anytime soon, especially as one child is now a pilot. Her other great love is Freddy, the "I think I'm a lap dog" Bernese Mt Dog.

Carolyn is also a Devo Writer, and co-author of Christian Marriage:

Devotionals from Both Perspectives.
Amazon (US) link: https://amzn.to/3XJbJV0
Universal Book link: https://www.bklnk.com/B0BSWDFSGG

Carolyn, having herself been transformed, wants passionately to share her tools of success, including how to cope with change, stop running and hiding from your past, overcome trials, and *become the best you* while growing lasting relationships. Her desire is for you to experience the *certain hope* she has.

You can journey with Carolyn:
Instagram carolyn.deck
FaceBook https://www.facebook.com/carolyn.deck
Email: c.deck4405@gmail.com